star power

"When I was hosting a recent Emmy-viewing party at my home, I wanted to have a fabulous grand prize for the winner. I had received many amazing gifts from Lash over the years whenever I presented at any number of award shows, so I knew he would be able to create the perfect gift assortment. He assembled a prize package that was diverse, fun and a total hit."

— JENNIFER LOVE HEWITT, ACTRESS

"The day I met Lash was the day my gift-shopping drama disappeared! I want to give people new and exciting gifts with a high 'ahhh' factor . . . yet something that feels personally chosen for them. Lash helps me find that unique and perfect item for my discerning colleagues, friends, relatives and even my kids!"

— HOLLY ROBINSON PEETE, ACTRESS

continued . . .

New American Library
Published by New American Library, a division of Penguin Group (USA) Inc.,
375 Hudson Street, New York, New York 10014, USA
Penguin Group (Canada), 90 Eglinton Avenue East, Suite 700, Toronto, Ontario M4P 2Y3,
Canada (a division of Pearson Penguin Canada Inc.) • Penguin Books Ltd., 80 Strand,
London WC2R 0RL, England • Penguin Ireland, 25 St. Stephen's Green, Dublin 2, Ireland
(a division of Penguin Books Ltd.) • Penguin Group
(Australia), 250 Camberwell Road, Camberwell, Victoria 3124, Australia
(a division of Pearson Australia Group Pty. Ltd.) • Penguin Books India Pvt. Ltd., 11
Community Centre, Panchsheel Park, New Delhi - 110 017, India • Penguin Group (NZ),
cnr Airborne and Rosedale Roads, Albany, Auckland 1310,
New Zealand (a division of Pearson New Zealand Ltd.) • Penguin Books (South Africa)
(Pty.) Ltd., 24 Sturdee Avenue, Rosebank, Johannesburg 2196, South Africa

Penguin Books Ltd., Registered Offices:
80 Strand, London WC2R 0RL, England

First published by New American Library,
a division of Penguin Group (USA) Inc.

First Printing, October 2005
1 3 5 7 9 10 8 6 4 2

Copyright © R. Lash Fary, 2005

NEW AMERICAN LIBRARY and logo are trademarks of Penguin Group (USA) Inc.

LIBRARY OF CONGRESS CATALOGING-IN-PUBLICATON DATA

Fary, Lash.
    Fabulous gifts: Hollywood's gift guru reveals the secret to giving the perfect
present / Lash Fary.
        p.   cm.
    Includes bibliographical references.
    ISBN 0-451-21657-1
    1. Gifts.   I. Title.
GT3040.F37   2005
394—dc22   2005010189

Set in Goudy
Designed by Jennifer Ann Daddio

Printed in the United States of America

PUBLISHER'S NOTE
While the author has made every effort to provide accurate telephone numbers and Internet addresses at the time of publication, neither the publisher nor the author assumes any responsibility for errors, or for changes that occur after publication. Further, publisher does not have any control over and does not assume any responsibility for author or third-party Web sites or their content.

This book is lovingly dedicated

to my best friends

jackie, arianna, jl and elisabeth

You each remind me every day that

the most fabulous gift of all truly is

priceless . . . your extraordinary friendship

is the wind beneath my wings.

acknowledgments

My undying gratitude to Marcy Posner and Krista Parkinson . . . because you're only as good as your amazing agents! A special thanks to Claire Zion and Tina Brown (and everyone at Penguin/New American Library) for believing in this project and for making my first publishing experience such an incredible pleasure. To The Recording Academy and Cossette Productions . . . thanks for entrusting us with the GRAMMY gifts year after year and for putting us on the map!

To Barbra Streisand . . . you epitomize everything an idol should be and set the standard for greatness.

To Mom and Paula . . . your support, faith and love are gifts beyond words.

To all my friends, who have been so enthusiastically supportive and have provided the inspiration for so many of these fabulous gift ideas.

My sincerest appreciation to my extraordinary team at Distinctive Assets for your hard work and dedication over the years.

And to my business partner, Todd West . . . you so humbly let me shine and so bravely join me on this journey. Carpe diem.

contents

introduction

I've always loved presents! Even as a child, I adored the mall and would pick up fun gifts for friends and family whenever I saw something special that reminded me of them. It was only a matter of time before I figured out a way to turn my passion into a career.

From the Oscars to the GRAMMYs, celebrity gifting has become a pop culture phenomenon . . . and my company, Distinctive Assets, helped pave the way. Over the past few years, Distinctive Assets has established a reputation for impressing the seemingly unimpressible Hollywood celebrity. Our roster of famous clients is nearly endless. Suffice it to say that if you've heard of them, we've probably gifted them or given a present on their behalf. But for the record, some of my personal favorites have been Bette Midler, Sharon Stone, Marc Anthony, Justin Timberlake, Heather Locklear, Megan Mullally and Ricky Martin.

The immense press exposure I received for creating lavish presenter and performer gift baskets at major award shows led me into corporate gifting based on sheer demand. Corporate America rightly assumed that if I could please J.Lo I could probably satisfy their clients and employees. Giving a present to a celebrity is remarkably similar to gifting your neighbor, aunt or accountant, and this book will show you how to do it with flair.

In *Fabulous Gifts*, I will provide you with the help you need to pick out terrific presents for everyone on your list. I can't do my own taxes or a back handspring, but I can give great gifts! And after reading this book, so will you. Over the years, I've been on many television shows talking about gifts . . . what I've given to celebrities, what stars like to buy, gifting trends, ideas for gift presentation, common mistakes in gift acquisition and gift etiquette. Now, all of that information is available to you in a succinct, easy-to-use format designed to share the simple steps involved in star-quality gift giving.

One of the cornerstones to giving the perfect present is to *know your audience*. If I am creating a gift basket for Paris Hilton, I always include an item or two for the one long-term love of her life: her dog Tinkerbell. If Debra Messing is being gifted, I avoid anything made of wool or cashmere (she's allergic). Salma Hayek, Alicia Silverstone and Pamela Anderson are all animal rights activists, so that eliminates leather and fur. Jennifer Lopez loves to be surrounded by things that are white. I've learned that knowing the personality of the recipient, their interests, hobbies, favorite colors and idiosyncrasies is crucial to successful gifting.

The key to giving a thoughtful gift is so conspicuous that it's often overlooked. Know what it is? The answer is so obvious that it's part of the very word itself: *thoughtful* . . . meaning, quite literally, "full of thought." However, many people don't take the time required to brainstorm about the gifts they give in order to come up with a surefire blueprint for a great present. Instead, they resort to thought*less* gifts that were acquired at the last minute, selected out of desperation and carelessly wrapped. But that is nothing a little planning, knowledge and creativity can't fix!

To that end, I've devised a quick quiz to help you get started. Once you've defined the "giftee," I'll suggest gifts in each of three price ranges for multiple occasions. I'll also share some presentation tips and wrapping ideas that will make your present stand out before it's ever even opened.

This book is *not* an alphabetized listing of every possible gift to give. It is a systematic approach to assessing the personality of your recipient and then swiftly implementing my personal gift-giving techniques. I'm sharing specific ideas that have worked well for me over the years in the hopes that you will be inspired in (and by) the gifts you give. Never again will you have to resort to that dreaded heart-shaped box of chocolates or (insert appalled sigh here) a fruit basket. I couldn't possibly discuss every conceivable gift idea, and you'll certainly discover hundreds of wonderful options on your own when you're out shopping. My primary goal is for you to recognize the perfect present when you see it and take advantage of the fact that you've found it. In a way, it's like learning algebra. Once your math teacher explains the basic steps in how you solve for x in an equation, you can do it over and over again in an infinite number of mathematical scenarios. To use that ancient proverb: "Give someone a fish, you feed them for a day. Teach them to fish, you feed them for a lifetime." You'll be getting both fish and fishing lessons!

You'll also have the help of dozens of fabulous magazines that provide gift guides in nearly every issue (often even categorized by recipient), countless catalogs that have already done much of the legwork for you and hundreds of buyers for stores across the globe whose sole job is procuring amazing new merchandise. You just have to start paying attention and develop a plan to methodically acquire all the gifts you need. With a little preparation, you will begin to experience one of the most satisfying pleasures in my life: having that perfect gift sitting in your closet, all the while bursting with anticipation to give it because you know how much the recipient is going to love their present.

Just as every gift represents an individual expression of you *and* the recipient, every occasion has its own unique qualities and challenges. Often, these occasions extend beyond the conventional one-on-one exchange. Group gifts (which happen to be a specialty of mine) range from weddings, showers and dinner parties to gifts in the workplace. The approach here is a little different, but my suggestions will make your shopping a lot simpler.

It is often said that it is better to give than to receive. I'm not sure that it is better, but it definitely taps into a different emotion. It is *exciting* to receive gifts; it's *joyful* to give them. I'll discuss ways to explore and expand upon the joy you experience from giving . . . to individuals, to organizations and to yourself.

fabulous gifts

chapter one

know
your
audience

Just as stand-up comics adjust the specific details of their jokes based on the age, sensibility and even geography of their audience, in order to give a fabulous gift you, too, will need to conduct a little background research on the recipient. Most people for whom you'll ever need to acquire a present will fall into some very basic categories. Part of avoiding the angst and pressure associated with buying a gift is to have a simple system in place in order to tackle the challenge head-on. The easiest tool I've found in my professional gifting life is to identify the basic personality type of the recipient and then brainstorm about gift ideas within those "personality parameters." Before I make a gift recommendation to any of my clients, there are three questions I ask them about the person for whom they are shopping:

1. *Is the giftee young (at heart) or mature (at any age)?* Being young at heart has nothing to do with the person's chronological age. Your grandmother might be spontaneous, free-spirited and adventurous . . . making her "younger" in terms of her shopping profile than your conservative niece who's destined for the convent. The same frivolity and joie de vivre that people bring to their daily lives should be reflected in the gifts you buy for them. Likewise, you'll need to be aware of and respect the seriousness and predictability of the more mature individual.

2. *Are they traditional or trendy?* The traditional individual tends to take fewer risks and feels more comfortable with the familiar. The trendy giftee is more daring and interested in what's new and exciting. The critical distinction here is separating your personality as the buyer from the inherent nature of the person for whom you are shopping. Traditional people tend to gravitate toward buying only traditional gifts, while trendy folks often step too far off the curb when shopping for their traditional counterparts. This is one of the hardest

impulses to overcome when establishing your gifting prowess.

3. *Is your relationship with the person that of a close friend or relative, or more of a casual, neighborly nature?* The closer you are to the person the more you'll already know about them. Although this will save you time in "researching" and "profiling" the individual, it also increases the probability of your becoming lazy and careless. In Hollywood, they say you're only as good as your last movie. In the wonderful world of gifting, you're only as good as your last gift. Approach every present as evidence of your thoughtfulness, creativity and talent. Consider it your mission to convert the raw data you have acquired through years of conversations into customized solutions. The more casual the relationship, the more challenging it becomes to find a gift that will be appreciated without seeming generic; this situation often demands sound judgment and good taste.

On the fence about any of the above classifications? If so, take a few moments to answer *yes* or *no* to the questions listed below. They've been engineered to help refine your perceptions about the person for whom you are shopping.

Please note that you may know the person well enough to skip this step. For example, you may identify without a moment's hesitation that your sister is *young* and *trendy*. In other instances, you might be gifting someone whose profession or hobby supersedes this personality typing altogether—meaning you may be selecting a present based primarily on a career theme rather than a personality profile. If that's the case, jump right in and let the creative juices start flowing. If you're lucky enough to be in either of these situations, you've been given a big head start.

Also keep in mind that the point of this questionnaire is not to narrowly define or pigeonhole an individual who might be a complex blend of all the attributes mentioned. It's simply an effective means of focusing your brainstorming efforts to come up with the perfect present.

YOUNG AT HEART VS. MATURE

1. Do they usually dress up for Halloween?
2. Do they enjoy telling jokes, making people laugh and playing pranks from time to time?
3. Do they have HBO?
4. Have they hosted a dinner or cocktail party at their home sometime in the past six months?
5. Is the recipient likely to drop everything for a last-minute weekend trip?
6. Would they join you for a spur-of-the-moment dinner or movie invitation?

7. Do they sometimes impulsively buy items they don't need while shopping at the mall?

8. Are they likely to join their coworkers for happy hour after work?

9. Are they likely to have to search for their passport when it's time to take a trip?

10. Are they more likely to stop at Starbucks for a latte in the morning than to set the timer on the coffeepot the night before?

11. Are they more likely to decorate the bride and groom's car at a wedding with shaving cream and toilet paper than to stay behind to toss the rice or birdseed?

If your answer to six or more of the above questions was *yes*, you're shopping for someone who is *young at heart*. If most of the answers fell into the *no* category, your gift recipient is *mature at any age*.

Shopping for someone *young at heart* means you'll be able to take more risks and have more fun with your purchases. If you're gifting a more *mature* individual, stick to the more practical side of things. As with anything, there are no absolutes, and your intimate knowledge of the person will always override a stereotype.

TRADITIONAL VS. TRENDY

1. Do they think about "other people's rules" when dressing (e.g., not wearing white after Labor Day or whether a particular color is appropriate for the season)?
2. Do they avoid tight-fitting clothing?
3. Are they more likely to watch CNN than Fox?
4. Do they go to church or temple on a regular basis?
5. Are they more likely to work around the house on the weekends than to hit the mall with a friend?
6. Do they read the newspaper every day (or on a regular basis)?
7. Does the recipient listen to either classical or country music?
8. If female, does she own more flats than stilettos? If male, does he own more neckties than pairs of jeans?
9. Has the recipient had the same hairstyle for at least five years?
10. Is the recipient often influenced by family opinions and situations?
11. Does the recipient own only black and/or brown shoes?

If your answer to six or more of the above questions was *yes*, you're shopping for someone who is *traditional*. If most of the answers fell into the *no* category, your gift recipient is *trendy*.

Buying a gift for someone who is *traditional* is in many ways an easy task, because they tend to like what they know and appreciate it when you give them something familiar. Purchasing a present for someone who is *trendy* can be a totally exhilarating shopping experience since they love bold colors and innovative ideas. Plus, *trendy* giftees are always willing to take fashion and design risks; this makes them the safest group for whom you'll buy a gift because almost anything goes.

CLOSE VS. CASUAL RELATIONSHIP

1. Would they be willing to pick you up at the airport during rush hour on a Friday evening?
2. Do you know their favorite movie, actor or singer?
3. Can you recall their birthday (or at least birth month) without referring to a calendar?
4. Would the recipient stop by without calling first?
5. Do you chat on the phone or exchange e-mail with the recipient at least twice a week?

6. Do you have the person's phone number programmed into your cell phone?
7. Do you have a picture of them in your house?
8. Do you share details about your sex lives with one another?
9. Do you socialize (outside of work) at least once a month (or at least talk about doing so)?
10. Would you feel comfortable going lingerie or underwear shopping together?
11. Would you leave them alone in your house for the day?

If your answer to six or more of the above questions was *yes*, you're shopping for someone with whom you have a *close bond*. If most of the answers fell into the *no* category, you and the gift recipient share a *casual relationship*.

The vast majority of the gifts you buy will be for people with whom you are *close*. It is important to get to know their gift preferences well and to become familiar with their hobbies, interests, favorite colors, career choices and passions. You'll only improve your gifting performance and ratings! The presents you buy for those with whom you have *casual relationships*, however, can be vitally important, as they often encompass business associates, clients and other individuals who have the potential to affect your livelihood. The impression you leave may well be quite critical and long lasting.

Based on the above data, you'll be shopping for one of the following types of people (think of this as the Myers-Briggs of gifting):

1. Young/Traditional/Close
2. Young/Traditional/Casual
3. Young/Trendy/Close
4. Young/Trendy/Casual
5. Mature/Traditional/Close
6. Mature/Traditional/Casual
7. Mature/Trendy/Close
8. Mature/Trendy/Casual

I have devoted one chapter to each of these personality profiles. I will lay out gift ideas for both men and women in two distinct categories: *personal gifts* and *romantic gifts*. Personal gifts are appropriate for birthdays, Christmas/Hanukkah and Mother's/Father's Day, while romantic gifts are suitable for more intimate occasions—namely, Valentine's Day and anniversaries. I will also suggest housewarming/host(ess) and baby gifts. I have not included weddings as a separate occasion since they are one of the rare times when couples make a nice and tidy list from which you're supposed to choose (something I recommend people do more often for any occasion). You simply select the item from their registry at your desired price point. There's no room for error. If you're a rebel and want to venture out on your own, my housewarming and anniversary gift ideas often make equally great wedding presents. You'll find that you can also extend my specific ideas and general strategies to encompass your needs for a variety of other occasions. Many of my suggestions can be used as get-well presents, gifts for athletic coaches at the end of a season, graduations, bar mitzvahs and so on.

Now it's time for the fun part . . . shopping!

People often wrongly assume that because I shop for celebrities the gifts I give must be astronomically expensive. Fear not, my friend. The entertainment industry is often just as budget-conscious as you or I! So I'll be providing you with fabulous choices in three different price ranges for each gift category.

> *Inexpensive: $25 and under*
> *Moderate: $25–$100*
> *Expensive: $100 and above*

I'll also include some *lavish* gift ideas here and there that may be more fantasy-based, unless you've recently won the lottery or starred in Paramount's latest summer blockbuster. They are meant for inspiration and fun.

You'll be able to adapt many of my suggestions to your local resources as well as to the uniqueness of the lucky recipient or event (including group gifts and professional occasions). Sometimes people make it easy for you by being obsessed with a particular person or area of interest: Barbra Streisand, butterflies, *The Great Gatsby* or African art, to name just a few. This will allow you to creatively pursue interesting ways to showcase the object of their affection: a European version of a movie poster they love, limited editions, vintage collections, coffee table books related to the subject matter, coffee mugs with their idol's picture on it, and on and on. Think of my ideas as a canvas with a masterpiece sketched in pencil . . . you'll be able to fill it in with your favorite colors, erase some lines to create your own images or simply trace over mine like a paint-by-number kit.

Also keep in mind that you'll want to read all the suggestions in all categories, as most of them make equally great gifts for multiple occasions. With a little tweaking for the person in question, you can make many of the ideas work for almost anyone of any personality type. Consider all of the following gift recommendations a mere starting point . . . a basis for brainstorming . . . a catalyst for a lifetime of fabulous gift giving!

chapter two

wit & wisdom
of gifting

I've given and received thousands of gifts over the years. There have been hits, misses, successes and . . . lessons. All of the advice I'll be sharing with you has come from firsthand experience and reflects my personal approach to giving the perfect present. Although there will be tips and insights sprinkled throughout the pages of this book, here are a few pearls of wisdom that will whet your gifting appetite and provide a solid foundation for my subsequent gift suggestions.

bag it and tag it.
When you find something that's either on sale or well suited for someone spe-

cial in your life . . . **Buy it! Wrap it! Tag it!** If you think to yourself, "That would be perfect for so-and-so," that means it is.

everyone loves an upgrade.

Some of the best gifts you'll give will be ones that upgrade an everyday experience . . . like drinking coffee, walking the dog or watching television. So make a list of things the person does habitually, and then start brainstorming about ways you can provide an enhancement!

raison d'être.

Presents should serve a purpose. You'll notice that very few if any of the gifts I'll suggest are mere clutter. Always ponder how the gift will impact the recipient's life. This is also a great exercise as part of your brainstorming process. Say you're shopping for a graduation present for your nephew. Ask yourself how he'll use the gift at college; if he is graduating from college, what will he need for his new job? But don't make this an overly strict standard. After all, simply providing beauty in someone's home is certainly a noble enough purpose for a gift!

candy's gift room.

Establish a "gift area" in your house. While yours may simply be a shelf in your closet, you may be interested to learn that Candy Spelling has an entire room in her Beverly Hills mansion dedicated to this purpose. Stock it with ribbon, wrapping paper, boxes, gift bags, tissue paper and note cards. Having the proper tools and building blocks is a critical foundation for success. Making one trip to a party store (or ordering in bulk from a Web site) is so much more efficient than running out at the last minute to buy these supplies on a piecemeal basis. It will also eliminate the stress, hassle and frustration of not having what you need when you need it. **Food for thought:** When you're at home, and all you have in your cupboard is junk food, that's what you eat. But if your refrigerator is filled with fresh fruits, organic produce and lean meats, the probability increases that you'll cook a healthy and delicious meal. It's really the same with your gift room . . . a well-stocked gift room is more likely to result in beautifully wrapped presents.

the final word on regifting.

Regifting is totally acceptable with the following caveats: You keep track of who gave you what so you don't make the supreme faux pas of giving someone back something they gave you (or giving it to someone with whom they socialize). In general, regifting should take place with people outside the circle of friends of the original giver, and out-of-state regifting is always best. Also, make sure you unpack and repackage the item in case a personal note was slipped in. You can never be too careful! It's definitely worth rewrapping a present just to be safe.

gift with purchase.

Whenever you order something for yourself from a catalog, find one other item that will make the perfect present for someone on your gift list. It will allow you to form a good habit of systematically checking off required gift purchases early. Plus, you'll save money on shipping charges; a second item will almost always have a much lower (if not free) shipping cost per unit.

you vs. them.

When you are shopping for someone (especially women shopping for their husbands or boyfriends), don't necessarily buy what you like . . . buy what they'll like. Analyze the items in the giftee's home and wardrobe when determining their predilections. After all, people know their own preferences better than you ever will. Gifts are not the time to impose your personality on others. Don't worry. You'll have plenty of other opportunities for that! Of course, there are exceptions to every rule: If your renowned style and taste might help them overcome an unfortunate penchant for the unattractive and unflattering, by all means intervene. It's like rehab through gifts.

our policy on returns.

Never buy an article of clothing that can't be returned or exchanged. If the store has a "no returns" policy, simply walk out and find one that accepts returns. It's always nice to include a gift receipt issued by the store with any gift of clothing. The only exception to this rule is if the perfect item is available on sale for such a steal that it's worth the risk of a "final sale."

good things come to those who wait.

Almost all stores (even the fancy ones) have amazing sales at least twice a year—usually in January and July—so take advantage of that fact by shopping then. You'll get a lot more for your money, and the recipient will think you spent more than you did.

take advantage of any holiday sale.
Stock up on holiday-themed serving bowls and other seasonal decorative items the week after the holiday (and not just Christmas). You'll be able to get them at least 50% off, and you'll be prepared for the following year's gift needs. These types of items make fantastic presents and will help keep you way ahead of schedule.

the little black book of gifting.
Create a database of the personal statistics you collect over the years. If you use Outlook on your computer, simply add such information as shoe sizes, birthdays, anniversaries, allergies and children's names to the "details" section. Otherwise, document the same information in a journal for easy reference.

extreme clothing shopping.
Whenever you are buying clothing as a gift for someone, stick to "extremes": *extremely* basic or *extremely* unusual. This way, you're more likely to hit the usability bull's-eye. You can't really go wrong with "basics," and even the most "unusual" fashions will be appreciated when a specific opportunity arises.

fake it till you make it.

If you can't afford to make that splurge purchase, find ways to either simulate the experience or extract elements that will at least provide a taste of the real deal. Substitute sports cars with model cars, expensive purses with key chains or wallets by the same designer, an exotic destination with a souvenir from that country.

stockpiling.

Always have standard gifts like candles, wine and champagne in reserve. Buy an entire case of wine (twelve bottles) at a time so you'll have it on hand for last-minute dinner party invitations. You'll save money because cases of wine are normally discounted about 10% off the per-bottle price. You'll also save yourself the trouble of running last-minute errands.

the bottom line.

Set reasonable budgets and don't overextend yourself or create a situation where you will later feel resentful that you spent too much on someone's present. The price tag is less important than whether or not you chose something thoughtful, interesting and special. There are so many small gifts that can be beautifully presented and accompanied by a lovely card that will serve your purposes perfectly. Of course, there are occasions and situations when it's definitely strategic to bite the bullet and splurge on the gift . . . for clients, for a best friend or for a special anniversary.

the card stash.

Stock up on cards. Don't just buy the ones you know you'll need; get a number of generic birthday cards and blank cards that are perfect for any number of occasions. Remembering someone with a lovely card can often be gift enough (or at least buy you time to follow up with a proper present at a slightly later date).

pay attention.

If you pay attention to your day-to-day conversations with friends and family, they will divulge a great deal of useful information about what they like and need. When someone talks about how much they loved a movie they just saw at the theater, make a note to buy them the DVD when it is released. If they compliment a piece of jewelry you've worn, get them something like it. If they repeatedly ask to borrow something of yours, buy them one of their own.

attendance policy.

I have no idea what Emily Post has to say about it, but I'm creating a new rule in baby gifting: If you give a baby gift at a baby shower, you do not need to give another present when the baby is born (unless you are a godparent, doting aunt or just want to). It's one gift per occasion/event. Similarly, if you don't attend a wedding shower, you aren't required to send a gift in your absence; that's only true of the wedding itself. A graduation or bar mitzvah invitation also necessitates a gift regardless of actual attendance. But remember, you should never give a gift unless you want to. More important, if you've been invited to an event and you experience resistance to the notion of buying the person a present, the person doing the inviting should probably reevaluate their guest list . . . and you might need to take a hard look at your "friendship."

the convenience factor.

Keep in mind the circumstances under which someone will be receiving your present. If they have to take a plane to return home after the holidays, give them gifts that will be easily packed but not easily broken.

write it down.

If you use a pocket PC or other handheld electronic device, take advantage of the event notification feature by programming in your friends' and family members' birthdays and anniversaries. If you don't have a PDA (personal digital assistant), make sure the right person knows about this technology deficit so they can buy you one for the next appropriate occasion. An hour of your time on a rainy Saturday will save you a lifetime of embarrassment for forgetting someone's special day. If you're not that technologically inclined, make it a New Year's Day ritual to take out your desk calendar and write in all the important birthdays and other noteworthy occasions for the year. Don't make the mistake of thinking you'll magically remember these things . . . it's simply not possible. Take my advice and write it down!

gift registry.

A gift registry is not just for brides and grooms. Take advantage of creating your own wish list for major personal occasions. Every Christmas my friend Jackie and I swap our wish lists so that we can guide mutual friends who ask about gift suggestions for the other party. It's a great way to get what you want! I also recommend keeping a gift registry at one or two of your favorite stores and simply telling anyone who asks, "What do you want for your birthday?" where you're registered. One of my favorite episodes of *Sex and the City* is the one where Carrie registers at Manolo Blahnik. She sends out an announcement that she's neither getting married nor having a baby but that she *is* celebrating being single and fabulous.

investing in a relationship (literally).
The longevity of your relationship is an important factor when shopping for your significant other. In newer relationships, you want to do something impressive, but because the odds are against you, it's probably not prudent to invest too much too soon (sorry for the jaded approach). You might want to save particularly extravagant gifts for milestone anniversaries (marriage or otherwise). In the beginning, impress with your thoughtful romanticism rather than the price tag. A little research will go a long way in finding that perfect gift . . . one that adequately reflects the time and energy you put into the selection process. If necessary, ask their best friend some pointed questions about their favorite places and things.

just say no to tacky bows.

Never use those awful little premade self-adhesive bows. No matter how many you put on the package, they are unacceptably tacky.

romantic appliances?

Never give your wife or girlfriend an appliance as a gift. To clarify, if cooking is her personal hobby, a deluxe mixer is no longer classified as an appliance. Vacuum cleaners, washing machines and any other devices used to clean up after *you* are *always* considered appliances.

a donation has been made in your name.

Although I'm an advocate of philanthropy, never give someone a "charitable donation made in their name" as a present . . . unless they've specifically asked for it, or it's a personal passion of *theirs*, whereby the gesture will be meaningful *to them*.

Armed with this knowledge, let us now boldly embark on our enchanted and magnificent gift journey. . . .

chapter three

young/
traditional/
close

Finding personally significant gifts that address practical needs in a fun way is the key when shopping for the *young/traditional/close* individual on your list. Many of the presents I suggest will be things they might consider buying on their own but somehow talk themselves out of for one reason or another. Other gift ideas will add scintillating variety to their daily routines and recurring needs.

FOR MEN

Personal Gifts
[for Birthday/Christmas/Hanukkah/Father's Day]

Inexpensive

The *traditional* man will always appreciate something as practical as dress socks since he uses them nearly every day. With so many fun designs and colors available everywhere from department stores to the Gap, you'll have plenty of options in every price range. Although I've spent as much as $85 per pair for designer socks at high-end department stores, I usually purchase dress socks when they are on some sort of "Buy 2, Get 1 Free" type of sale. I've never found the inflated price differential to be justifiable. Go the bargain route . . . you'll be able to get multiple pairs and remain within your budget. Remember, these men are also *young at heart*, so don't be afraid to stray from the solid black or blue options. There is something very liberating about wearing dramatic socks with a conservative suit or outfit. It's the perfect balance for the *traditional* man who enjoys expressing his *youthful* spirit.

Moderate

Whether he wears it with a suit to work or with jeans on the weekend, a new dress shirt makes a wonderful gift for a *traditional* man of any age. One can really never have too many, and with practically limitless options you'll be able to find a color or print that speaks to his *youthful* sense of style. Stick with Egyptian cotton for comfort and get the best label you can while staying within your budget. Keep your eye out for sales whenever you're at the mall, as this is the type of item that is perpetually on sale somewhere. Because this is not particularly seasonal merchandise, you'll be able to cross a dress shirt off your list anytime. I'm on a personal quest to rid the world of the très passé button-down collar, so please take my fashion advice on his behalf and avoid this frumpy style choice.

Expensive

This type of man is *traditional* and, therefore, understands the value of wearing a nice timepiece. Because he is *young at heart*, he'll like having yet another option in his watch repertoire. Finding a sporty watch in the $100–$200 range is totally doable, and your gift of a casual watch will be ideal for weekend use . . . especially if you choose something interesting like a brightly colored band, a leather cuff style or a diver's model. I've given fun, sporty watches with a retail price of less than $300 to dozens of celebrities who wear them with great zeal. I've run into both George Lopez and Kenny Loggins backstage at award shows, where they've pulled up their sleeves to reveal that they were wearing the sport chronographs I had given them nearly six months earlier.

If the recipient's personal taste is more formal, you may end up paying a bit more for a nice brand-name timepiece, but fortunately the Internet provides great deals on both luxury brands and antiques. You might also have great luck at estate sales and pawnshops; the history of the timepiece will appeal to his sense of *tradition*. Plus, you'll avoid paying retail for a brand name at a fine jeweler. You're typically better off going with something that is slightly used rather than settling for an economical dress watch with a less than prestigious brand name.

Lavish

In a town where "bling bling" has become du jour, watches in Hollywood can easily become *lavish* purchases with the addition of a few carats' worth of diamonds. Although I have several watches, my favorite is a *less expensive* variation of one owned by P. Diddy (Sean Combs). Every time I look down at the diamond-encrusted face and see it sparkle in the sunlight, I feel special and on top of the world. So if your budget allows, make his day with a fabulous watch! And if diamonds aren't his thing, there's no *traditional* man out there who won't appreciate having a Rolex on his wrist . . . which will definitely set you back a mortgage payment or two.

Romantic Gifts
[for Valentine's Day/Anniversary]

Inexpensive

Boxers or briefs? It's an age-old question. Regardless of the answer, the price tag will surely be under $25. Since this occasion is all about sex, romance and love, you'll be both thematic and practical with this gift choice. Most of the popular designer underwear brands are always coming out with new styles, provocative cuts and festive colors, so this is a great opportunity to satisfy the adventurous element of his *youthful* personality.

Plus, you'll receive the fringe benefit of having him model the gift for you!

Moderate

The *young traditional* man will certainly have a recreational activity of preference—be it golf, tennis, racquetball, running or cycling. Take a trip to a specialty store for that particular activity (or an all-encompassing sporting goods store if you have one in your area), and you'll be presented with a world of options. From portable golf putter sets (includes sectional putter, golf balls and aluminum cup) and unique cans of tennis balls (try customizing with his initials or favorite expression) to new cycling helmets and waterproof running gear, you'll be able to create a gift, or an array of gifts, that will address his athletic interests. Items like the portable golf putter set are great because they are easily transportable for use at home, the office or even a hotel.

Expensive

Depending on the make and model you choose, purchasing "his & her" bicycles is *expensive* at best but can easily become a *lavish* present. This creative gift is both impressive and boasts what I call the "I totally love this and never would have bought it for myself" factor. His *youthful* side will dig that it's action-oriented, while his *traditional* nature will revel in the romanticism of the sunset biking excursions you'll enjoy together. The point of this gift isn't necessarily to buy the newest, most *expensive* and most impressively aerodynamic bike out there (unless, of course, your *young traditional* man is actually a biking enthusiast who would appreciate those features . . . in which case I recommend dropping the "her" part of the gift and buying just one nicer "his" unit). Whatever you do, don't carry the idea of cycling together too far by purchasing one of those two-seater bicycles. If you decide to do that for fun sometime, just rent a doubles bike at the beach for the day. Don't invest in one though; they are remarkably impractical and will likely be something you'll only want to use once. This gift concept works equally well for skiing, snowboarding, ice skating, surfboarding, Rollerblading or any other activity you'd enjoy doing together.

FOR WOMEN

Personal Gifts
[for Birthday/Christmas/Hanukkah/Mother's Day]

Inexpensive

Ranging from classy to kitschy, there are so many interesting options when it comes to toiletry and lingerie bags that you'll be able to address her *youthful* personality and interests while catering to her *traditional* need for organized and hygienic travel. The even better news is that you can find these ever-useful travel bags at discount chains across the country. Your goal is to discover something she'll appreciate aesthetically rather than something of such high quality that it will last a lifetime. For example, one of my best actress friends loves anything leopard, so I bought her one of those expandable hanging travel toiletry bags in a leopard print. Whenever I visit her on the set, it's there in her dressing room, and she never fails to mention what a perfect gift it was. It didn't matter that I got it off the $10 clearance table at Marshalls!

Moderate

I've given decorative pillows for the living room, study or bedroom with great success. The *traditional* side of this giftee will welcome the additional accent for her home, while her *youthful* spirit will love the sense of fun in breathing new life into an established room. The general rule of thumb would dictate a set of two, but an individual pillow can be totally acceptable— especially if you go with an unusual material such as suede, sheer floral, metallic or my all-time favorite . . . feathers. Indian embroidery is typically as beautiful as it is affordable. Believe it or not, it's often more difficult to incorporate a solid blue or beige pillow into a room than one made of abalone shells or peacock feathers. If it's festive, bright or ethnic, it will add an interesting touch without having to exactly match the upholstery.

Expensive

Nearly everyone is eternally frustrated with their closet. There just never seems to be enough room for everything! Although there are companies who will come in and redesign her closet so that it will look like Karen Walker's on *Will & Grace*, you can achieve a very similar result on a much more modest budget. There are quite a few stores that offer do-it-yourself ways to maximize closet space. With a combination of shoe shelving, hanging canvas sweater organizers and basic compartment boxes, you'll be able to create a surprise for her that will delight and inspire. This can be an all-at-once project or something you divide over a number of gifting occasions. Keep in mind that any individual closet reorganization component is equally great as a stand-alone gift without the "installation" element. I recently acquired new shoe shelving for my closet (for right around $125) that makes me smile every morning when I open the closet door. Odds are so will she!

For an alternative with similar benefits, consider providing the necessary tools for a kitchen reorganization: shelving units, drawer trays, chef carts, cookware caddies and counter racks.

Romantic Gifts
[for Valentine's Day/Anniversary]

Inexpensive

Luxurious bubble baths and scented bath oils make a lovely and *inexpensive* gift for the *young traditional* female. There are many preassembled gift sets that also include a loofah and bathtub headrest, or you can easily create your own (using the basic gift basket assembly techniques I discuss in Chapter Fourteen). This is a highly accessible gift, as you'll be able to pick up the required elements anywhere from a drugstore to a beauty supply chain.

Moderate

Lovely lingerie will surely please the *young traditional* woman. The nature of her *"traditions"* and the extent of her *"youthfulness"* will determine whether you go racy or classy. You always want to stick to colors and styles that are flattering for her body type and will make her feel beautiful and alluring, not silly and self-conscious. If you wait till the last minute on this, you'll definitely have to pay full price. If you take advantage of the after-Christmas sales, however, you'll get a lot more for your money. Remember that Valentine's Day is a lot closer to Christmas than you might realize at the time!

Expensive

Flowers are certainly not a novel gift, but there's something irreplaceable about the beauty they create and the romance they inspire. Their appeal is universal, perennial and intoxicating. I simply never tire of receiving a stunning arrangement of fresh flowers. In order to make this *traditional* present even more impressive and to up the ante as a stand-alone Valentine's gift, I suggest expanding the idea of giving her flowers *for the occasion* to giving her flowers *for the year*. It is easy to create a standing order with your local florist to have a simple bouquet of flowers delivered each week or once a month. You'll save money by having them delivered as an unarranged bouquet rather than a floral arrangement. If you have the discipline to stick to a pickup schedule, you can further economize by picking up your own bouquet at your local market (or flower mart if you're fortunate enough to have one nearby), and bringing them home to her on a regular basis. Every woman is likely to have her favorite flower (for Halle Berry, it's white roses), but don't feel obligated to get her the same thing every time. In fact, save "her favorite" for truly special occasions so they will stand out. For all those other times, go with what speaks to you. . . . Often, it will be whatever is in season, as those blooms tend to display the boldest and most vibrant scents and hues. My favorites are lilies, tulips, lilacs and daffodils. For the most part, keep it simple by sticking to a single variety each time. Respected style mavens have waged a successful smear campaign against baby's breath and carnations, so you'll want to stay away from this taboo flora.

If you want to avoid the ongoing effort of regular deliveries, you might consider filling her apartment or office with flowers. This onetime act will achieve a similar result by using a *traditional* gift to make an extraordinary statement. It will require *a lot* of flowers to pull off the intended effect, so make sure to buy an overly sufficient quantity when implementing this option.

FOR HOME

Housewarming/Host(ess) Gifts

Inexpensive

Coasters come in all sizes, materials and price ranges. Keep the recipient's décor and personal taste in mind when you're determining whether to go with an animal print, a hunter's lodge feel, art deco or solid. You can even make your own coasters if you are artistically in-clined and have a Home Depot or art store nearby that sells stone tiles. Simply buy the square tiles and add let-ters or images using a paint pen or actual paintbrush. Stencils are particularly helpful for this project. If you're going the "homemade" route, words with four or five letters work best: L-O-V-E, P-E-A-C-E, S-M-I-L-E or even the person's last name if it's short enough. An object, or series of objects, with personal relevance functions equally well.

Similarly, packages of cocktail napkins provide equal charm and great bang for your buck. If you plan ahead, you can even have monogrammed or personal-ized napkins created quite affordably. You'll have plenty of options under $25, and your gift can be used either for seasonal occasions or year-round.

Moderate

How many times have you had to borrow a card table from a neighbor or friend for entertaining purposes? **Things you find yourself in need of on a regular basis make terrific gifts for others.** Whether they use it as the "kids' table" at a large dinner party or for that weekly poker game, having a card table around the house will surely come in handy. An upgraded variation of the card table is an actual game table. Often these tables are designed to be multifunctional, have all sorts of fun drawers with storage space and are ideal for card and board games.

Expensive

One of the gifts for which I continue to receive the most effusive thanks is the picnic basket. The picnic basket is the perfect example of something everyone loves conceptually, but most people don't own. You can go deluxe or basic, wicker or canvas, fully lined or exposed rattan, two-person or four-person. The deluxe sets will include such items as a blanket, thermos, plastic containers with lids, cutting board, flatware, plates and glasses. You can also just add your own accoutrements to a *less expensive* basic picnic basket on an à la carte basis, depending on your budget. This also makes a functional and elegant wedding gift.

FOR BABY

Baby/Baby Shower Gifts

Inexpensive

With newborns, visual stimulation is known to spark creativity and intellect. There are dozens and dozens of crib accessories, ranging from playful mobiles to glow-in-the-dark constellations that can be affixed to the ceiling. Handcrafted toys from an exotic land will fill the baby's crib (and imagination) with wild tales of far-off destinations: cat dolls from Peru, stuffed wool farm animals from Mexico or rag dolls from Argentina. This international toy/doll idea can be the genesis of a collection you supplement year after year.

Consider other collections you might originate for the child. Aunt Vi initiated my one and only bona fide collection by giving me the annual "proof set" (coin set) issued by the U.S. Mint every year since I was born. She also started my fascination with Christmas tree ornaments by instituting the tradition of adorning my Christmas present each year with a homemade ornament from her church bazaar. To this day, I lovingly place each and every one of those ornaments on my tree. Whether your gift remains with the child for a week or a lifetime, choose objects that will soothe, excite, inspire or amuse.

Moderate

Studies show that reading to babies both prenatally and postpartum increases their comprehension and verbal skills (something the *traditional* mother will surely have read all about). I love to give expecting or new parents books on varying topics. Whether an illustrated classic or a celebrity creation (both Madonna and Jamie Lee Curtis have published children's books), your gift will be used at a formative time in the child's life and will look lovely on the parents' bookshelves for years thereafter. One of my favorites is a children's story-time book that comes packaged with an adorable "sleepy star" nightlight . . . which can be found in many celebrity nurseries, including Shania Twain's, Martina McBride's and Reese Witherspoon's.

Expensive

Nurseries are an ideal place to explore stimulating colors and *youthful* decorations. A piece of furniture that will be a perfect accent to the nursery and equally enjoyed long after by the *young at heart* parents is a beanbag-type chair. There are updated versions that retain their shape much longer thanks to an innovative and patented foam filler. Most of these contemporized beanbags have interchangeable covers. Once the nursery becomes a teenager's bedroom and eventually a guest room, new covers will allow the beanbag to change with the times. These chairs are great for cuddling with baby and beyond.

Lavish

Kids absorb everything around them, and numerous studies have examined the role that a child's surroundings play in its emotional development and stability. Customized designs can foster a unique and engaging environment that supports the emotional well-being of a child. Animated characters, personalized decorative furniture and original artwork are just a few of the tools that can be integrated into a nursery or bedroom by a qualified professional. This is a truly remarkable present for children with special needs stemming from ADD, ADHD and autism. However, every child can benefit from this extraordinary gift. Even if this type of consultation isn't in your budget, seek out books published on this topic. You can give them as gifts so that parents can explore the benefits of using color and art on their own.

chapter four

young/
traditional/
casual

The *casual* nature of your relationship means you may not possess much of the firsthand information needed to truly customize, so you'll want to stick with more tried-and-true gift ideas. These "basics" will be useful yet still incorporate something a little unexpected and exciting. This represents the perfect balance for a fun-loving, *youthful* spirit tempered by the practicality of a *traditional* perspective.

FOR MEN

Personal Gifts
[for Birthday/Christmas/Hanukkah/Father's Day]

Inexpensive

A mini gumball machine is the perfect desk accessory for the man who is *young at heart*. He can fill it with his favorite candy or gum, and it provides a splash of color to an otherwise bleak set of desk accessories. We've used this gift idea quite successfully for a number of our corporate gifting projects involving *traditional* male executives and have always received rave reviews.

Moderate

If he already has a power toothbrush, he'll love having another one for traveling or to keep at the office. If he hasn't discovered the wonders of this advancement in oral hygiene, this might be the best gift you'll ever give him. You can pick these up in a broad range of prices, depending on whether you go battery-operated or fully electronic. They even have integrated models now that dispense their own toothpaste! Not only is this product amazingly convenient, but you'd be hard pressed to find a dentist who wouldn't tell you that it provides a much deeper clean.

Expensive

Although you may not be able to buy him a Porsche, why not splurge for the next best thing: Porsche driving shoes ($365–$485). These handmade Italian leather driving shoes come fully equipped: flexible black leather uppers, anatomically arched footbeds and specifically designed padded heels that allow for well-balanced thrust. The name alone is steeped in *tradition* yet evocative of speed, excitement and *youthful* exuberance. Getting his shoe size should be an easy task, but if it proves problematic, you might opt for a radio-controlled Ferrari instead. This replica offers real speeds of over 24 mph and a true racing experience for the car buff on your list. Depending on the make and model, this type of toy will cost between $100 and $200.

Lavish

It's truly out of the pages of *The Lifestyles of the Rich and Famous*: Hop on a private jet in New York and land in Paris for a romantic dinner, followed by a Sting concert at the Zenith Arena. Okay, so you're not Jennifer Lopez and Marc Anthony, but you can still adapt this type of *lavish* luxury enjoyed by quite a few celebrities to your own degree of extravagance. Fly commercial to an out-of-town destination to catch a performance that simply won't be in your area. Rent a convertible and go on a weekend road trip to a nearby city that is hosting the concert he loves. Book that trip to Tahiti you've been talking about. The key to capturing the essence of any over-the-top celebrity indulgence is to lose your concept of "boundaries" when making plans. Expand your horizons and think bigger in every possible way. Don't settle for going to your favorite local eatery on Saturday night. Instead, drive an hour to a neighboring city and try a new restaurant that you read about in the newspaper. Replace practicality with an open-minded, adventurous spirit.

FOR WOMEN

Personal Gifts
[for Birthday/Christmas/Hanukkah/Mother's Day]

Inexpensive

There's something about a girl and her diary that women who are *young at heart* never seem to outgrow. Her musings may be random thoughts, poetry or even "to do" lists, but a beautiful journal is a gift a *traditional* woman of any age will love. There are so many lovely and unique journals available everywhere from stationery chains and paper boutiques to photography stores. Some of the most stunning journals I've given as gifts have been bold-colored leather with a wraparound tie clasp, accordion-style folding parchments made of natural-colored raffia (a favorite of Sandra Bullock), and imported Italian works reminiscent of the Old World. Journals can also be used as photo albums, depending on the design. Although you could easily spend over $100 for an embossed leather journal, there are many designs that will still delight her for under $25, especially if you stick to a "diary" size. Even if the giftee doesn't write on a regular basis, you'll give her an excuse to start. I've actually used some of the beautiful journals I've received over the years as ledgers of sorts to maintain important lists and financial documentation or to jot down random inspirations. It enables me to keep this information at hand on my desk in a very aesthetically pleasing way.

Moderate

The *traditional* woman typically enjoys the nurturing aspect of cooking for her friends and family. That being said, her adventurous inner *youth* relishes the discovery of new recipes, side dishes and preparation techniques. So enroll her in a weekend cooking class (or series of classes) at a local culinary school. Many gourmet kitchen supply chains also offer such courses. If you don't have access to this sort of thing, there are numerous cooking DVDs and videotapes that will accomplish the same goal.

Of course, any number of classes make great gifts. If cooking isn't her hot button, investigate dance classes. Whether it's salsa, ballroom or something in between, it's a great tool in terms of both presentation and gift content to also include a DVD of *Dirty Dancing*, *Shall We Dance* or a classic like *Singin' in the Rain* (or even a

CD like Lee Ann Womack's *I Hope You Dance*). If dance isn't the ticket either, continue to brainstorm until you find an area of interest she'd love to pursue, such as astrology, learning a foreign language or an introduction to playing the stock market.

Expensive

Laptop bags have come a long way since the days of boring black suitcase-looking tote bags, and you'll be able to find them in a lot more places than just a luggage or computer store. Why not reward her with a fabulous laptop bag that will double as a briefcase or even carry-on? These bags come in many beautiful designs and in all sorts of color schemes. I like to give laptop bags that are constructed of nice leather in a basic solid color on the outside but are bright and colorful on the inside. Although she'll be using it for work and other *traditional* purposes, whenever she reaches inside she'll smile at the fanciful splash of color . . . which will appeal to her *youthful* nature. Avoid nylon and other cheap materials that will make your gift look like something you picked up at a work seminar.

FOR HOME

Housewarming/Host(ess) Gifts

Inexpensive

I entertain a lot and find that having herbal teas (translation: no caffeine) available for my guests is always a welcome addition to the expected offering of coffee. Herbal teas are great to have on hand for after-dinner conversation and late-night socializing. If you haven't yet discovered it, try jasmine-flavored tea. Herbal teas are also a convenient gift item, because they can be found at most grocery stores. Tea is usually packaged nicely already, but you can make your gift more impressive by placing assorted varieties in a pretty basket or by purchasing a tea caddy, which has a number of compartments to keep the teas organized. The tea caddy may be a little harder to find but is well worth the hunt. I've found great ones at Bombay Company, World Market and even Costco.

You can easily substitute a canister of gourmet hot chocolate (in a lovely decorative tin) or fresh ground coffee. "Gourmet" hot cocoa means it came from a chocolate specialty store and *not* from a generic super-market. When bringing fresh ground coffee to a dinner party, I recommend decaf. An exception to the decaf rule occurs if you also bring as your gift a mini basket of muffins or coffee cake for your hosts' breakfast the next day; in that case, caffeinated coffee will be a better accompaniment. I always suggest buying ground coffee; don't bring whole coffee beans unless you know with absolute certainty that your hosts have a grinder. And if they do not have a coffee grinder, take note, as that will make a wonderful gift down the road.

Moderate

Wine is a standard option when visiting someone's home for dinner or for a housewarming event. Many of our corporate clients cannot be convinced to stray from this tried-and-true gift. So if you can't beat 'em, make it better! Placing the bottle in a wine box or wine tote adds an extra layer to your gift that is sure to make it stand out. Totes and boxes come in all sorts of materials: wood, leather, canvas and rattan. With a little research and input from a wine professional, you should be able to find a respectable bottle of wine at a very reasonable price . . . allowing enough room in your budget for the carrier. Wine boxes are usually made to accommodate single bottles, while many wine totes will allow for two bottles. If you purchase the two-bottle variety, I always recommend pairing a red with a white.

You can transform wine into a truly spectacular gifting experience if the recipient is a film buff or has an obsession with a particular movie icon. One of my prized possessions is a limited-edition bottle of wine with a picture of Barbra Streisand on the label. There are similar "icon collector's series" of Cher and Marilyn Monroe. If you've truly overplayed the wine card with a particular recipient, try giving a fabulous wine accessory like a vacuum pump corkscrew, an educational wine-tasting kit or a lovely book about wine.

Bringing *inexpensive* wine to a dinner party isn't the end of the world. If you're gifting a wine connoisseur or an important client, though, make sure you cough up at least $25 for a slightly nicer bottle. And be sure to ask the wine merchant for assistance. If you're winging it at the grocery store, play the odds by opting for an Australian or French varietal.

Expensive

Traditionalists frequently surround themselves with their friends and loved ones and, therefore, entertain often. A beautiful crystal vase, bowl, decanter or carafe will be used repeatedly for years to come. Unique shapes, colors and beveled designs are typically the most interesting, but classics are fine, too. Larger vessels are more risky (but if you're confident in your taste, they can be a year-round accent in the person's home). Although you'll find eye-catching crystal items that would fit into either the *inexpensive* or *moderate* category (especially if you live near an outlet mall), I recommend reserving this for more of a high-end gift, because cheap crystal will reflect poorly on you and create a potentially awkward situation for the giftee if they don't want to use it. My general rule of thumb is to ask yourself whether you'd display the item in your own home. **If something is below your own standards, you should never give it as a gift.** Feel free to explore serving bowls and accoutrements that aren't crystal as well. Craftspeople around the world design items that will brighten any table, so add an international flair to your present by seeking out French porcelain, Swedish glass and Indonesian bamboo. I speak from experience when I say that people who entertain can never have too many bowls, platters and vases.

When buying a housewarming or host(ess) gift around a holiday (and not just the big ones), choose a holiday-themed serving item. It's the type of thing that

is so gratifying to have in one's seasonal decorating re-
serves, but so totally annoying to buy for oneself since
it's used so rarely.

FOR BABY

Baby/Baby Shower Gifts

Inexpensive

Bibs get so messy so fast, parents can never have too
many. So get as large a set as your budget will allow. I
love giving the plastic-coated kind that can be wiped
down easily. Fun prints, stripes and polka dots are all
great design options.

Moderate

Memory boxes often look like elegant books from the
outside, but when the lid is opened there's space for
storing favorite mementos and photos. You can engrave
many of these boxes with the child's name, either on a
brass plate or directly onto the wood. Whether it's kept

on a shelf or displayed on a coffee table, the memory box will remain a sentimental favorite for years. Although a number of stores in many malls across the country carry these, you can also create your own simply by engraving and affixing a plaque to an antique box or chest of almost any material or design.

Expensive

Most parents want to take every precaution when it comes to looking after their newborn, including "eavesdropping"—for safety reasons—whenever they have to step away from the nursery. Giving parents a portable audio monitoring system will allow them to listen in on the baby even when they are in another room or in the yard. Putting a parent's mind at ease is a priceless gift, and these can be found in any baby boutique or department store.

chapter five

young/
trendy/
close

The *young/trendy/close* giftee is an interesting one, for you should know them well enough to make bold yet personalized choices. They love anything creative, different and cutting edge, so you've literally got a world of possibilities. This is perhaps the most forgiving category for which you'll shop because almost anything goes. Even if you make a misstep, you're *close* enough to be allowed leeway in the "what were they thinking?" department. You should have as much fun shopping for this type of person as they have with the gift you give them.

FOR MEN

Personal Gifts
[for Birthday/Christmas/Hanukkah/Father's Day]

Inexpensive

This present is called a "hangover kit," and you'll want to reserve this for people with whom you are *close* because it is a bit personal and cheeky. It is one of the most original items ever included in our award show gift baskets. Although it was created by an online pharmacy for the 44th Annual GRAMMY Awards, I have adapted it with great success for many *young trendy* partiers in my life. You start out with a lunch box of any kind . . . this is where knowing the person relatively well will come in handy, because you can get one with their favorite childhood cartoon character, action hero, entertainer, musical group or recent movie. For example, anyone creating this gift for me would surely find a Wonder Woman lunch box. You can even go with simple aluminum if you're feeling stumped (think of it as "industrial chic"). You'll then proceed to fill it with all the items one would need to function after a night on the town: headache medicine, breath mints, bottled water, toothpaste, toothbrush, protein bar, eye cream for puffiness, eye drops and antacid. I've even included things like baseball caps, sunglasses and T-shirts. All of these items are available at your local drugstore. You'll win praise for your creativity, and you'll receive additional thanks down the road when the giftee actually needs to dig in.

A variation on this clever gift is the "911 Emergency Supply Kit" for the car or home, complete with a mini flashlight, bottled water, dried fruit, candles, matches, flares and first aid kit.

Moderate

Because this man is both *young at heart* and *trendy*, he's likely to embrace fashion more than the males in some of the other categories. So why not pick him up an appropriately fabulous garment from his favorite store or designer? Even high-end designers have affordable yet stylish items in their lines. This *trendy* giftee will also like the statement made by his label of choice. It could be something simple like a great pair of jeans (if you're sure of his size) or an amusing T-shirt. Don't be afraid to experiment with an unusual color or unique detailing.

Expensive

Mini stereo systems have seen great technological advances in recent years. The units are smaller, and the sound is bigger. All of the major stereo manufacturers offer desktop/portable/micro models ranging from $125 to $500. It's perfect for a home office, garage, guest room, nightstand or rec room. Some units include alarm clocks and are even compatible with MP3 players. A super add-on (or replacement gift if you're looking for something in the same family with a smaller price tag) is a pair of noise-reduction headphones; there are "comfort" models that are effective and, as the name implies, oh-so-comfy.

Romantic Gifts
[for Valentine's Day/Anniversary]

Inexpensive

Coolers are a practical amenity for *young* and *trendy* guys who are likely to take day trips, join their friends for sporting events and enjoy lazy afternoons at the beach. I particularly like the compact sizes for this purpose. Some coolers even have features like built-in radios, which provide added fun. Finish off this gift by including his favorite microbrew or other beverage of choice. He'll just need to add ice and hit the road with his buddies.

I've found that a larger cooler can also make a great housewarming gift, as it comes in handy when defrosting the refrigerator or when having larger social gatherings (for ice, extra food storage, etc.).

Moderate

Trendy men aren't afraid to wear jewelry. Whether a simple silver necklace, chunky thumb ring or sexy leather cuff, he'll think of you every time he wears the item. You're looking for stylish accessories, not a wedding band, so stay out of *traditional* jewelry stores; this will also keep the price down. Flea markets, artisan bazaars and specialty clothing stores are a better source for affordable merchandise with a casual and hip flair. If in doubt, use his favorite male musician(s) as your inspiration. Musicians tend to be *trendy* and have access to fabulous jewelry. Peruse magazines featuring these gentlemen, see what they're wearing and track it down. One of my favorite pieces of jewelry was inspired by a rosary-style necklace Ricky Martin wore to the Latin GRAMMY Awards. I commented on how much I loved it, and one of my attentive friends gave me one just like it for my birthday that year.

Expensive

Buying that special man in your life art may seem like a daunting task, but it can be a superb way to provide a lasting reminder of your love throughout the year. Whether the recipient resides in a house or an apartment, there is almost always a space on a wall crying out for a new piece of art. You have a number of different options here, depending on your budget. There are great framed prints available at most home accessory stores. If the giftee has a favorite movie or actor, ordering a vintage poster online and having it framed for his office or study is a thoughtful gesture. Be even more creative by going online to find a European movie poster of the same film. You may also want to check out new, up-and-coming talent at art exhibitions and street fairs . . . you'll get much more for your money and might even stumble upon the next Picasso in the process. You'll want to stick to colors, themes and frames that work in the recipient's home, so start paying attention to some of the following details before starting to shop: Does he have silver or gold accents and fixtures? Are most of the existing frames wood or metal? What are the primary and accent colors in the room(s) in question? Is there a particular theme in art already established that you can continue or enhance?

Recognizing my status as a *young trendy* man, one of my best friends recently took this bold step and was the first person who dared to buy me a piece of art. It was a butterfly painting by the renowned artist Hunt Slonem. Because my friend is much better versed in the world of art and knew I wouldn't be familiar with Hunt, she also included a beautiful coffee table book about the artist. This way she ensured that I would truly understand the value of the gift I had received. The painting's colors and frame style were perfect for my bedroom, where it was immediately hung.

If you find an original piece of art that is simply too *expensive*, ask about reproduction options. My business partner remarked once how much he loved a particular piece of art we had seen together. I really wanted to buy it for him, but it definitely wasn't in my budget. Because the gallery owner knew how much I coveted the painting, she recommended the gyclée process. This is a method of computer-generating a reproduction, which is then printed directly onto canvas (usually by the artist), so it appears much more authentic. Not as cheap as a typical reproduction, but remarkably *less expensive* than the original painting. Where there's a will, there's a way.

FOR WOMEN

Personal Gifts
[for Birthday/Christmas/Hanukkah/Mother's Day]

Inexpensive

Women in this category tend to pay close attention to the details of their appearance and are thrilled by any form of pampering. Therefore, the *young trendy* female likely invests in regular manicures and pedicures. I've found that people are always appreciative when they receive a gift that saves them money on an activity on which they are going to spend cash anyway. I certainly don't have any medical research to back this up, but I'm convinced it releases endorphins into your system when you can enjoy one of your regular pamper treatments and then whip out a gift certificate to pay for it. Stop by her favorite local nail salon and pick up a gift certificate for either a manicure or pedicure (or both if you're fortunate enough to live in an area where the pricing allows). Alicia Keys and Sharon Osbourne loved the complimentary manicures and pedicures we gave them backstage during rehearsals at the 46th Annual GRAMMY Awards, so we sent the nail technicians to their hotel and home, respectively, to touch them up for the actual ceremony the next day. That's a celebrity's version of a mani/pedi gift certificate!

Moderate

Women in this profile group are also fashion mavens, so you're sure to elicit a gleeful and giddy response with any sort of clothing item. Simply visit her favorite store and select a top, blouse or T-shirt. I recommend staying away from pants and skirts, as sizing is much more difficult to bull's-eye, and women tend to be more sensitive than men about receiving the wrong size. If the garment is too tight, they'll feel fat; if it's too large, they'll think you perceive them to be bigger than they are. It's a no-win situation you'll want to avoid if possible. Ask the sales clerk about hot new arrivals, as *trendy* women will receive extra delight from that.

Expensive

Since I launched Distinctive Assets back in 1999, we have always used luggage to house all of the wonderful gifts we give to stars at award shows. From the beginning, the response to this easy-to-transport "gift basket" was overwhelmingly positive. As he was preparing for his ill-fated space mission, Lance Bass was seen on CNN wheeling around the piece of Tumi luggage he had just received from us at the GRAMMY Awards. Jill Scott and Bonnie Raitt loved the luggage we gave them and called to acquire additional pieces to complete their sets. Whether you add a new piece to the recipient's existing luggage, start a new collection or provide a stand-alone duffel to be used for the gym, the giftee will surely find the perfect use for her newest accessory. In this day and age, almost every style comes with a pop-up handle and wheels, which is ideal for traveling. Stick with versatile colors, but don't be afraid to stray from primary tones.

Lavish

Luxury luggage toted by many celebrities can cost as much as $10,000 for a single piece. Multiply that by five or six (carry-on, garment bag, train case, large-wheeled carryall, etc.), and you end up with one *lavish* gift. For those of us who don't have a Julia Roberts budget, you don't have to treat someone to the entire set of luggage at once. Simply build it up over time until they have all of the pieces they desire.

Romantic Gifts
[for Valentine's Day/Anniversary]

Inexpensive/Moderate/Expensive

Jewelry, jewelry, jewelry. I'm so adamant that this is *the* way to go when shopping for a woman in this category that it's going to be the only option I recommend. In addition to being the ideal gift for this occasion, jewelry is a viable alternative no matter what your budget. As always, the more you can spend the more choices you'll have. The good news is that the *young trendy female* loves fun and funky accessories, which tend to be more affordable. Budget-conscious shoppers should concentrate on things like amber rings, woven African bracelets, crystal toe rings, glass bead necklaces and string necklaces with unique findings. You do tend to get what you pay for when it comes to jewelry, so if you're on a tight budget, find something special and unique that will serve as a conversation piece.

A *trendy* stone like turquoise runs the gamut, from very *expensive* to very *inexpensive*, depending on the designer and the stone's quality. What you might be lacking in bling you'll make up for in sentimentality if you can link your jewelry purchase to a trip or fond remembrance . . . for example, "I got you this hand-carved wooden bangle bracelet because it reminded me of that trip we took to Morocco last year." Remember, the more clever you are the less you'll have to spend. One year I stumbled upon the perfect gift for the poster girl for the *young trendy* woman: Debra Messing. It was a simple silver chain with five small uncut precious and semiprecious stones (uncut stones are *much* cheaper): *g*arnet, *r*uby, *a*methyst, *c*itrine and *e*merald. It was called the GRACE necklace because the first letter of each stone spells out that word. For the star of the hit show *Will & Grace*, I couldn't have thought of a more perfect gift. More important, Debra loved it.

If you have a bigger budget, bear in mind that any woman loves diamonds and platinum! Spend some time investigating various cuts and settings and find a way to involve her in the process. There are entire books dedicated to shopping for diamonds, and for the uneducated I recommend using your local jeweler's expertise as a free tutorial. If you covet the look of precious stones but don't want to max out your credit card, here's the not-so-awful truth about cubic zirconium: When going the route of cubic zirconium or other simulated stones, stick with a simple cut and design. For example, a heart pendant with pavéed cubic zirconium stones will make a much classier (and believable) presentation than a ring with one large or gaudy imitation stone in it. This is one of the rare occasions where less is more. A pair of $300 simulated diamond stud earrings is going to work better than a $500 version of the million-dollar *Titanic* necklace. Plenty of costume jewelry looks fabulous, is ideal for travel and makes a perfectly acceptable gift . . . if you choose wisely.

I have found that many magazines do an amazing job of finding unique jewelry lines and specific pieces that epitomize the hottest trends. After all, it's the job of those accessories editors to be on top of what's new and exciting. So let them do the work for you. Flip through some of the top women's magazines and you'll have countless incredible options served up to you on a silver platter. All of these magazines cover jewelry in a range of price points, so you'll be able to find something whatever your budget. They usually even list the phone number of the store where the piece is available, so you may never have to set foot in a mall if you don't want to. No matter what you spend, the fact that you made the effort to personally pick something out for her will go a long way.

Lavish

Celebrities are known for their *lavish* jewelry. Although they usually borrow those jewels for the red-carpet events you watch on television, the Elizabeth Taylor school of thought is "Why borrow when you can own?" You might recall the story of the 40-carat platinum and diamond custom-made Harry Winston princess necklace that Gwyneth Paltrow wore to the 71st Annual Academy Awards. After she won the Best Actress Oscar that year, her parents bought her the $160,000 necklace as a memento of the career-changing night. What a *lavishly* thoughtful gesture. If it's a special enough occasion, you might want to do some creative financing and take her breath away with a truly spectacular piece of jewelry.

FOR HOME

Housewarming/Host(ess) Gifts

Inexpensive

Your *young* and *trendy* host(ess) will enjoy the whimsical nature and creativity of fun and clever refrigerator magnets. Whether political, sexual or simply cute, stylish refrigerator magnets as a gift create one of my favorite sensations: the feeling of getting a present that you will totally use but would never have bought yourself. Refrigerator magnets are available at many stationery stores, kitchen supply stores and even some drugstores.

Moderate

Serving fondue is fun and delicious. Giving someone a fondue set is a nice addition to their entertaining arsenal and unusual enough that they aren't likely to already have one. Make sure it's enameled cast iron, so it won't burn and will be easy to clean. I also like to include a block of chocolate or cheese, so they'll have an incentive to break it in right away.

Expensive

The *young* and *trendy* are likely accustomed to eating out frequently, but it's awesome to help them revel in the joy of dining in their new home without having to do their own prep work. This type of present is a real treat because it is something people would rarely if ever do for themselves: hire a personal chef to cook them a meal in their own home. This will usually be billed by the hour, and depending on the stature of the chef can range from $50 per hour to $25,000 for the night. However, you can find eager young chefs (translation: affordable) who will be willing to accommodate this unusual request. If it's just not an option in your area or on your budget, simply order a complete meal and have it delivered to their home. This type of gift is historically reserved for people who are sick or recovering, but why not expand the courtesy to other occasions. An even more cost-effective way to achieve the same result is to prepare the meal yourself and deliver it just in time for dinner. One of the best barometers in evaluating your gift choice in any category is to put yourself in the giftee's shoes . . . how stoked would you be after a long day at the office to come home and enjoy a delicious dinner you didn't have to prepare? I've reserved this for *close* relationships because you need to know at least the basics of the person's eating habits, especially any restrictive diets you may need to accommodate.

FOR BABY

Baby/Baby Shower Gifts

Inexpensive

There are dozens and dozens of super-chic baby fashion companies these days. They have created clever baby T-shirts and onesies that are actually more fun for the parents than the children . . . which is really the point of most baby gifts anyway. For an affordable hit, find a baby tee with an expression or image that reflects the personality of either parent or child. One of the biggest sellers in our boutique is a line of baby tees that have fortunes from fortune cookies printed on them in red Chinese-style letters; they even come creatively packaged in Chinese take-out boxes. Oprah liked these unique T-shirts enough to give them to her friend Julia Roberts as a baby gift.

Moderate

A fashionable diaper bag can easily be a surrogate purse, and the *young trendy* mother will be pleased with as many options as possible. Explore fun colors and unique designs. Remember, it doesn't have to be called a diaper bag to be used for one. I'll never forget the picture in *Us Weekly* of supermodel Heidi Klum using her $6,000 Hermès purse as a diaper bag. Most purse lines carry large tote-style bags, which can easily double as a diaper bag and then later be cycled into mom's post-toddler wardrobe. From chic tweed to retro Pucci prints, the diaper bag has come a long way, thanks to the onslaught of fashionable celebrity moms like Gwyneth Paltrow, Kate Hudson, Reese Witherspoon and Liv Tyler.

Expensive

Having a baby seems to make you instantly sentimental and, therefore, a sucker for any symbolic gift. That combined with the positive environmental benefits of this next suggestion make it an unusual yet apropos gift for *young trendy* parents. Buy them a tree to plant in their yard (or nearby park) to commemorate the birth of their precious new child. Call a local nursery (the kind for trees, not babies) to find out the type of tree that will thrive in the particular climate where the gift will be given.

Lavish

A full-sized freestanding arcade game can be as fun for *young at heart* moms and dads as it will be for the kids. Although the child may have to wait a few years to play, it's a fanciful addition to the nursery. Stick to cult classics like Pac-Man and Gallaga, which seem to have greater longevity, and the whole family can enjoy it for years to come. Most of these arcade machines start at approximately $3,000.

chapter six

young/
trendy/
casual

Although the recipients here are daring and exciting in their style and taste, you may lack the personal rapport to be too risky or presumptuous in your gift giving. The likelihood of finding the perfect present will increase if you find ways to enhance their everyday experiences and cater to their penchant for luxurious convenience. This personality type is label-conscious and will appreciate the finer things in life. They are very likely to be familiar with Mae West's famous mantra "Too much of a good thing is wonderful."

FOR MEN

Personal Gifts
[for Birthday/Christmas/Hanukkah/Father's Day]

Inexpensive

The *young trendy* male is likely to make a morning "pit stop" at his coffee shop of choice for a latte, espresso, cappuccino, Americano or iced café. So give him the gift of a morning buzz! Every major coffee chain offers gift cards, and you'll be able to treat him to several mornings of caffeinated pleasure. Contrary to what some people will tell you, a well-chosen gift card or gift certificate is far from the "easy way out." (Money in an envelope is another story!) For the record, my friend Jackie *still* talks about the time I surprised her on the set of her TV show with a nonfat, no-foam, extra-hot latte with two Equals (her high-maintenance beverage of choice). So surprise him at the office or on Sunday morning with his favorite order. **Sometimes the larger part of your gift is the special effort you make.**

Moderate

One of the most stylish accessories a *trendy* man can sport is a cashmere scarf. A scarf in a basic color will be used often and looks great with everything from a cashmere or wool winter top coat to a jean jacket. It's especially nice around the holidays if the giftee has to travel to a frigid climate to visit family. If he lives where it's cold, he'll already have a scarf or two in his dresser drawer. In this case, opt for a more unusual color. For those guys who live in warmer regions, summer-weight cashmere makes the perfect lightweight accessory when there's that slight chill in the evening air.

While we're on the topic of cashmere, I should point out that it is perhaps the "most giftable" fabric. Everything about cashmere is special, which means even a basic commodity can be instantly transformed into a luxury item. Once you've given him a scarf, treat him to cashmere socks or lounge pants.

Expensive

A portable DVD player is one of the most popular gifts to give among our entertainment clientele, particularly record labels and studios. The prices vary depending on screen size, picture quality and brand. The good news is that even the *least expensive* models are still fabulous. It makes traveling so much more enjoyable, as the giftee is no longer limited to the movie selections offered by the airline, and the battery life is long enough for coast-to-coast travel. In addition, this is a great way to watch movies at home without leaving the warm covers of the bed (assuming he doesn't have a TV and DVD player in his bedroom already). This also makes a terrific "get well soon" gift for someone in the hospital.

FOR WOMEN

Personal Gifts
[for Birthday/Christmas/Hanukkah/Mother's Day]

Inexpensive

The lipstick caddy is one of the most ingenious inventions I've come across in recent history. If you aren't familiar with it, it's basically a box with individual compartments for assorted lipsticks. It keeps the dozens of tubes surely floating around her bathroom cabinet so organized she'll wonder what she ever did without it. They are available in small and large sizes, as well as numerous colors and patterns. We included leopard ones in our Latin GRAMMY presenter gift baskets, and I won great praise when I gave them to almost every *young trendy* woman on my gift list last Christmas. Many beauty supply stores will carry simple versions, and more unique styles can be found at novelty stores and online boutiques. This type of stylish organizational tool can be expanded to include cloisonné pillboxes, fun leather coin purses (I have one in the shape of a heart) and plastic or glass cotton ball/Q-tip dispensers.

Moderate

Young trendy women love to take care of their skin and will eagerly visit a local aesthetician for preventive maintenance. It's totally acceptable to buy a gift certificate to cover the basic facial offered by whatever institution you select and allow the person to upgrade with additional services if they choose. In fact, it's best not to select a specific type of facial for them, as the facialist should recommend this based on their current skin needs. If you don't have access to a reputable aesthetician in your area, create a nice assortment of face-care products from a **spa-quality line** . . . but don't shop at the drugstore for these. You can either go online or call the top spa in a major metropolitan area.

Expensive

MP3 players are all the rage, and even if the recipient already owns one, I've found you can always use additional units. I like to keep one by my bed, one in my gym bag and one at the office. That way, I'm never caught without this addictive device. There are various models offered by a few leading manufacturers. The primary factor that determines the price is the number of songs you can download. They now offer so many accessories and peripherals for MP3 players that you'll also create an opportunity for supplemental gifts down the road . . . like my bedside audio docking system that allows me to listen to my favorite playlists without headphones.

FOR HOME

Housewarming/Host(ess) Gifts

Inexpensive

I adore nightlights. I have lovely crystal nightlights strewn throughout my home. They add a touch of elegance and ambiance. I've given crystal nightlights, porcelain flower nightlights and nightlights with miniature paintings as illuminated façades . . . all with equal success. Your host(ess) will be able to use this gift in the hallway, bathroom, living room or bedroom. People rarely buy nightlights for themselves, but once they have one, they'll want several more . . . so don't be afraid to stock up.

Moderate

There are so many gorgeous coffee table books available at any bookstore (or finer department stores, such as Neiman Marcus, Barneys and Saks). Your hosts or new home owners will appreciate a beautiful book whether it adorns their coffee table or bookshelf. If you know anything about their specific interests, it will help narrow your search for the perfect book. In my case, I have a whole section on my shelves dedicated to the Barbra Streisand books I've been gifted over the years. Even if you know little about the person for whom you're shopping, a collection of distinguished photographs or a museum art book makes a lovely addition to any home. Be sure to inscribe the book with a personal message on the inside front cover that connects the theme of the book to the giftee. This will be fairly obvious if you know the person loves Katharine Hepburn and you give them a book about her. Even if it's a stretch, come up with something apropos. If I were invited to the home of someone I had just met and brought a pictorial retrospective of Impressionist art as my gift, the inscription might read: "Dear So-and-So, May your home and life always be filled with the beauty and inspiration found in these paintings."

Expensive

The *young* and *trendy* helped launch the luxury coffee franchise bonanza. Although they are likely to stop at a coffee shop for their double-shot mocha cappuccino, they'll welcome the ability to whip up and savor their favorite espresso beverage at home—especially since today's designs are so sleek, cool and aesthetically pleasing. Many espresso machines will easily slide into the *lavish* category, but there are single-cup models priced in the hundreds rather than thousands of dollars. If all of the espresso units you find are out of your budget, go with a coffee press and pair it with some gourmet coffee and a set of beautiful oversized coffee mugs. No regular brewed coffee tastes better than the coffee that comes from a coffee press. This is a gourmet item every coffee connoisseur will know and appreciate. Whatever your choice, discover some way to upgrade their coffee routine at home.

If coffee is not their thing, or you've already exhausted that topic, buy them an ice cream machine instead. These start at as little as $50 and go up in price from there. From the basic unit to larger frozen dessert and milk shake makers, this gift will bring out the kid in anyone . . . and result in delicious treats!

Lavish

Several of our vendors offer in-home espresso machines that are state of the art, easy to use and *very expensive*. We often have a $5,000 machine set up backstage at many of our award shows. Literally, with the touch of a button, our celebrity guests are enjoying a French vanilla double soy latte. The deluxe models tend to address the hardest part of in-home espresso preparation: steaming the milk. These units make foam with ease, offer simple cleanup and make the need to go out for your fancy coffee much less compelling. Denise Richards and Lauren Holly were both so smitten with the models they saw backstage, they bought units for their own homes; Denise actually bought four!

FOR BABY

Baby/Baby Shower Gifts

Inexpensive

It's *inexpensive*, unusual and sentimental . . . making it a perfect present for *young trendy* parents: name a star after the newborn. This is easily done online and provides a celestial map to pinpoint the location of the star you've selected as well as a certificate of authenticity. I recommend framing the certificate in a thematic baby frame with stars on it so that the gesture will be preserved for posterity and remain an interesting conversation piece.

Moderate

Plush baby blankets are often so decadent the parents might want to borrow them for their own evening television viewing. I've found that some of the most sumptuous blankets are actually made of polyester or polyester blends that feel more velvety than real velvet . . . yet they're machine washable! Who ever thought polyester could be so cool? I love choosing something a little edgy in its style/design. I've given camouflage-print blankets for boys and animal prints for girls. Sometimes I'll go with the time-honored pink or blue if the fabric is super-luxurious. Holly Robinson Peete opted for this conventional route when she gave a divine baby-blue velveteen blanket with satin trim to her friend Shar Jackson. When pictures of Shar cradling her son, Kaleb, appeared in *Us Weekly*, baby Kaleb was warmly and cozily wrapped in the fabulous blanket.

Expensive

Having an extra car seat always comes in handy, whether it's for the nanny, a babysitter, the grandparents or simply the second family car. If the parents don't have a car seat yet, they'll obviously need one. If they do have one, you'll save them the trouble of transferring a single apparatus from one car to another.

As an alternative, the *trendy* new mom will certainly covet the latest and most stylish baby carriage or papoose as well. Renowned fashion designers are coming out with all sorts of beautifully lined and trimmed strollers for as little as $299. Coordinate with a friend and have them give a matching diaper bag. (See Chapter Five for suggestions on diaper bags.)

chapter seven

mature/
traditional/
close

A common misperception is that *mature* + *traditional* = *boring*. Nothing could be further from the truth. The *mature traditional* personality type does gravitate toward the more predictable and less frivolous gift. But the good news is that the presents you devise for these types of people will become your "standards." You'll be able to use them over and over again, upgrading or economizing based on your budget. You'll even be able to give these "classics," with a few modifications, to people in other personality demographics. Think of your *mature traditional* gifts as Type-O blood (the universal donor). . . . Everyone can use them!

FOR MEN

Personal Gifts
[for Birthday/Christmas/Hanukkah/Father's Day]

Inexpensive

What is it about a man and his car? No matter the make, model or year, the *traditional* man is likely to take a keen interest in his "ride." If he's the type who likes to hand-wash his own vehicle, I recommend a nice car-cleaning kit packaged in a waterproof carrying caddy. If he's more the car wash type, find a car wash near his home or office and buy him a gift certificate for one or more complimentary washes. Most basic car wash packages start at about $10, so you can either include a couple or upgrade to a more deluxe detailing service. Either way, he'll love the gift!

Moderate

The *traditional* man is always a likely candidate for a sweater. But please do us all a favor and stay away from those terrifying prints and holiday snowflakes. After all, the goal of any gift is to actually improve the person's life and circumstances. A classic solid-colored cashmere or cotton sweater is the way to go. He'll have it forever and will be able to wear it around the house, while running errands or to the office. I prefer to give turtlenecks, V-necks or zip sweaters because they're a bit more interesting. Sweaters almost always tend to run on the baggy side, so try a more fitted cut or a size smaller than he'd wear in a shirt, especially if he'll likely wear the sweater under a suit. Cashmere can be pricey, but picking it up at the end of the winter season and setting it aside will allow you to stretch your budget and get more for your money. Remember to take proper moth protection measures when buying sweaters early. There are also wonderfully soft synthetic fibers that provide a nice (and *less expensive*) alternative to cashmere. I discourage wool unless it's a nice blend that feels soft to the touch.

Expensive

Whatever his favorite sport, an autographed item by one of the legendary players of that profession will likely become a family heirloom. Autographed MLB baseballs, NFL football helmets or NBA player jerseys can all be acquired and showcased in appropriate display casings. The respective players' association for each sport makes such memorabilia available for sale, and eBay is a great source of more obscure items. For the sports enthusiast, contemplate other splashy options, like season tickets to see his favorite local team or box seats for the next big home game.

Romantic Gifts
[for Valentine's Day/Anniversary]

Inexpensive

Shaving for the *mature traditional* male may well be the one and only step in his skin care regimen, so help him maximize it. I find this to be the easiest way to incorporate good facial conditioning habits in the lives of *traditional* men. Assemble an assortment of shaving creams, razor blades and aftershaves in a convenient travel bag; I recommend a coated or plastic inner lining in case of spillage. If they use an electric razor, it's still nice to have this type of kit for traveling, as a backup during power outages or simply for guests.

Moderate

Whether you give him his favorite cologne, your favorite cologne on him or a new scent that might become a favorite, nice fragrances (meaning $30 and up per bottle) make a safe and effective gift for the *mature traditional* man. I'm always delighted to receive my signature cologne, as I use it every day and love not having to go to the fragrance counter to purchase it. Many cities have "perfumeology" stores that will make custom fragrances for both men and women. You can develop a one-of-a-kind scent that incorporates his (or her, if you decide to use this for a woman on your list) favorite elements. Since this is a romantic day, include a note that punctuates the prevailing sentiment of the occasion. Write a message such as "I love the way you smell" or "Your scent drives me wild."

Don't be afraid to experiment with new colognes. I'm a staunch advocate of having gifts on hand for last-minute needs, so even if the recipient doesn't like the brand you've chosen, they can always add it to their gift closet to be used as a "regift." If you're completely stumped as to what fragrance to choose, go with two of the most versatile on the market: Acqua di Parma or Bulgari. They are light and classy.

Expensive

Men and their electronic gadgets . . . it's like peas and carrots. So give him a sleek compact digital camera, which is ideal for parties and for travel. These fun and colorful models can cost as little as $125. If he already has a nice camera, accessorize it! Buy him one of those photo printers, and he can simply insert the memory card to print his own lab-quality photos. Camcorders are fabulous, though pricier, options. Either way, the *mature traditional* man will cherish being able to capture magical family moments for posterity.

Of course, a cool new cell phone will always delight. No matter what current model he might have, he'll enjoy exploring all the bells and whistles of the latest version. Today's cell phones do a lot more than just make calls; they shoot video, take pictures, play music and organize your day. Although most of the cooler models are in the $250–$400 range, many carriers offer sizable rebates when you extend your service plan. If your budget doesn't allow for the phone itself, get him a wireless earpiece or keyboard plug-in for instant messaging.

If none of these items will appeal to the man for whom you're shopping, take a stroll through your local Sharper Image, Good Guys or Brookstone. There will be all sorts of recording devices and peripherals that will surely put a smile on his face.

Lavish

GPS systems come standard in many high-end automobiles. For the man who loves cutting-edge electronics but may not yet have that $80,000 car, this is an addictively useful present. Portable GPS systems are far more convenient than pulling up maps online, and this fabulous gift will allow him to avoid fumbling with folding paper maps in the car, and will save *you* hours of driving around lost with the typical male who refuses to stop and ask for directions. Pricey (starting at $1,299) with an equally high wow factor.

FOR WOMEN

Personal Gifts
[for Birthday/Christmas/Hanukkah/Mother's Day]

Inexpensive

Women (especially mothers) are predictably sentimental. I always try to find something nostalgic to
give my mom for occasions like Mother's Day and
Christmas—a gift that will remind her of me all year
long. One of our favorites was inspired by an artist
friend of mine who was doing some custom book il-
lustrations and bindings for a concept she called an "I
Remember" book. I gave her a list of a few dozen of
my favorite memories with my mom, plus any requi-
site backstory. She then came up with a fitting illustration for each one. The book was bound with
textured papyrus paper, given a thick card-stock cover
and embellished with raffia. Every memory had its
own page, custom font and corresponding illustration.
I wrote an inscription for the inside front cover, and it
sits on her living room coffee table to this day. I've

since adapted this as a birthday gift for my best friends and have recommended it for countless clients. Although my custom-published version cost a few hundred dollars, with a little ingenuity and time you can create your own for under $25! Simply purchase a lovely journal or binder that looks special or unique in a way that reminds you of the person for whom you're shopping. If you are handy with a word processor, you can play around with some of the more unusual fonts to create the actual "memory" pages. Then sketch some illustrations for each. If you're an artistic dud like me, try cutting out appropriate images from magazines or using some of your favorite photographs of the two of you together. Don't worry that it looks "homemade". . . . That's actually the point. If you have any calligraphy skills, go ahead and tackle the printing that way. Another version of this is to incorporate photos and favorite quotes into an inspirational custom-made photo album.

This is appropriate for almost any occasion, even as a memorial gift for someone who has lost a loved one. I also recommend that students change this to a "We Remember" book as a gift for a teacher at the end of the school year. Each student is responsible for creating a page commemorating their favorite memory of the year. All of the pages are then bound for a lasting keepsake that will be like that teacher's personal yearbook.

Moderate

Once again, sentimentality comes to your aid in shopping for the *mature traditional* female. Just as she'll appreciate receiving a beautiful greeting card, she's likely to send quite a few. Those of us who mail a lot of birthday, anniversary and "just thinking of you" cards throughout the year will love this idea, which was inspired by a Hallmark advertisement I saw for one of those handy dandy greeting card organizers. My adaptation is to pick up the organizer and proceed to *fill it* with assorted birthday and special-event cards. Be sure to include blank cards with lovely and versatile designs on the front. This will allow the recipient to be thoughtful all year long with the utmost of ease. This is a particularly wonderful gift for the elderly who have a difficult time getting out and about to run last-minute errands like picking up greeting cards.

Expensive

The pashmina . . . it's as timeless as denim. Although most women already have one or more of these in their wardrobe, some of the new design variations make smashing and ever-so-useful presents. My personal favorite is the pashmina with suede fringe. It's a unique twist on the original and complements denim, leather or cocktail attire with equal aplomb. Sharon Stone is a huge fan of this unique yet classic idea and has picked up quite a few as gifts. Actually, many of our actress clients have pashminas in every color, as they are ideal for red-carpet events . . . they provide warmth yet are easily removed for photo ops. Don't worry if you're not shopping for someone famous; these accessories are equally fabulous for church or even grocery shopping!

Romantic Gifts
[for Valentine's Day/Anniversary]

Inexpensive

For those of us who respectfully fulfill our thank-you note obligations (see Chapter Sixteen), fine stationery is always in need of replenishing. Of course, the *mature traditional* woman will have countless other occasions to use beautiful stationery. Your goal here is to select paper or note cards that have a lovely or unusual texture, boast an interesting detail or will be personally relevant to the recipient. My friend Liz is known for her note card etiquette and has given me some of the best stationery over the years:

- "L" initialed note cards (on heavy card stock) with color-coordinated lined envelopes and "L" initialed seals/stickers for the outside of the envelope
- card stock note cards with a sketch of the Hollywood sign on the front, along with my name
- linen paper (beige) trimmed in leopard

- blank cards with the Thomas Fuller quote "Good clothes open all doors" printed on the front

There are many local artists across the country who create unique greeting cards with poetic messages that are so beautiful and insightful it makes writing anything on the inside almost unnecessary. These inspirational messages are available at better card stores and online with minimal search effort. I find that bookstores are more likely than actual card stores to carry "special" note cards. You'll be able to purchase stationery alone *inexpensively*, but when my budget allows I like to include a roll of stamps, a set of colored fine-point markers and other writing accessories.

Moderate

If you aren't giving jewelry, the next best thing is a lovely jewelry box. Whether it's the type that sits on her dresser or a style designed for travel, I've always gotten a very positive response for this gift. You'll have a diverse selection from which to choose: mirrored glass, canvas, leather, wood, expandable models, armoires and many more. If the recipient travels frequently, I recommend a jewelry roll or a similar travel version, which you can pick up at a department or luggage store. You might even consider a strongbox or safe for her fine jewelry.

Expensive

Oprah has been quoted as saying if she only had one gift to give, this would be it. Based on the number of celebs who have purchased the *Together* CD collection for any number of occasions, I'd have to agree. It's beautiful enough to be a deluxe hardcover coffee table book because it includes lovely black-and-white photography as well as quotes from famous philosophers and poets. It also contains ten themed CDs of instrumental music spanning the decades and covering every musical genre. You'll find music for a romantic dinner or a soothing bath from artists as diverse as Barbra Streisand and the Beatles. It's music, it's poetry, it's art, it's thoughtful, it's sentimental, it's useful . . . and Oprah approves! What more need I say? This also makes a great host(ess) gift.

If you love this concept but the $150 price tag is too high, you can make your own version by simply buying an assortment of romantic CDs and combining them with a book of poetry or quotes. In this era of music downloading and CD burning, you can even make a modern version of the mix tape in the comfort of your own home.

FOR HOME

Housewarming/Host(ess) Gifts

Inexpensive

Discreetly tucked away here in the *mature/traditional/close* housewarming gift section is my all-time favorite gift to give and to receive. I'm often accused of being impossible to buy for (which is totally untrue!), but I'm here to tell you that for those of us who love candles, it's an insatiable obsession. Candles provide romance, ambiance, elegance, beauty and aroma. There are hundreds of varieties, scents and price points. My preference for both personal use and gifting is the glass jar form. Whether you give one significant candle or an assortment of lower-priced candles, you can make this gift work for anyone and for any occasion. I've given individually wrapped votives as party favors, created an extravagant "candle cornucopia" as a present for fellow candle addict Catherine Zeta-Jones, and added a personalized label for special occasions like weddings. Showing up with a great candle or set of tapers for the dinner table will be as appreciated by your host as a fine bottle of wine.

Moderate

Think of tablecloths, place mats and runners as fashion for your table. Would you want to wear the same outfit to every dinner party you attended? As with clothing, the options abound: solid, beaded, prints or even holiday-themed. If you've been to their home and know the color scheme of their kitchen and the shape of their table, you'll have a much easier time with the tablecloth option. Do not give plastic or vinyl tablecloths. If in doubt, go with a runner or place mats in lieu of a tablecloth. Don't worry that they already have one. Variety is the spice of life. More important, this type of item is highly susceptible to spillage and often needs to be replaced anyway due to permanent food stains.

Expensive

Potted plants last much longer than the dinner party you'll be attending and, therefore, make the perfect present. Large potted orchids have reached the pinnacle of classiness in recent years. The finest restaurants and spas often incorporate them into their décor. An orchid is elegant, attractive and versatile, as it will work in almost any room of the person's home. Orchids are my definite preference, but you can go with any potted plant that will appeal to the recipient's sensibilities. The peace lily, which is simple and durable, is also a great option and will cost you far less than a potted orchid. When giving a plant, be sure to include a nice pot and drain plate along with it.

FOR BABY

Baby/Baby Shower Gifts

Inexpensive

No parent can have too many pictures of their children on display. I'm not even a parent, yet I love receiving picture frames and photo albums as gifts. There always seems to be an "empty" spot on a wall or shelf calling out for a framed photo or, conversely, a great photo in need of a fabulous frame. There are many options, but I recommend finding frames that don't smudge or tarnish easily (so avoid silver). Similarly, no matter how many photo albums parents receive as gifts, they always seem to be full. Besides the obvious practical benefits, I love having beautiful photo albums on my bookshelves at home, for decorative value as well as nostalgia. As with any number of my gift suggestions, make sure your present has a little flair . . . created by a local artist, crafted with a unique design detail, made in an unusual color, and so on.

Moderate

A rocking horse or rocking chair makes a charming addition to any nursery. A rocking horse will serve as a creative room accent until the baby is old enough to play with it. A rocking chair is superfunctional and soothing enough to be used for hours on end. Its appeal is *traditional* yet timeless. A rocking chair can be moved to the TV room or even to the front porch and enjoyed well beyond the years of those fond memories of rocking baby to sleep.

Expensive

It was one of our biggest hits in terms of award show gift baskets, so I decided to start using it for our regular gifting efforts. At the 2002 Kids' Choice Awards, although the presenters were adults, our gift bag theme was "For the Kid in All of Us." So what better way to showcase all the presents than in a shiny red wagon! Everyone from Tom Cruise to Eddie Murphy wheeled theirs away from the event with a smile on their face (well, their assistants did the actual wheeling, but they supervised). And they were surely greeted by even bigger smiles when they got home to their kids.

Once you have your wagon, simply fill it with stuffed animals of all sizes and any other toys that are appropriate to the age and gender of the baby. I recommend buying a wagon that's preassembled if at all possible, as it's really not much fun putting these together . . . I say this after having to assemble over 125 for the Kids' Choice Awards. Don't worry about "wrapping" the wagon; because of its cumbersome nature, a simple bow on the handle is totally adequate.

chapter eight

mature/
traditional/
casual

What this category lacks in piz-
zazz it makes up for in accessibil-
ity. You'll find *casual* gifts for
mature traditional individuals almost everywhere you look. Your challenge here is not
coming up with a gift they'll like; it's sup-
pressing your urge to "keep looking" because
you don't think your original selection is exciting enough. In fact, if your thought is,
"This is a great gift, but it isn't terribly exciting," it means you've chosen properly for
this category. Often, the obvious choice is
your best choice. Don't overcomplicate shopping for the *mature traditional* giftees on your
list.

FOR MEN

Personal Gifts
[for Birthday/Christmas/Hanukkah/Father's Day]

Inexpensive

The *mature traditional* man is likely to appreciate a fine cigar. Individual cigars (packaged in glass tubes or otherwise) sell for about $25 and make a lovely impression. Of course, you can find cheaper cigars, but, as with wine, the reduced price will be reflected in the quality. You can buy packages of three for under $25, but I recommend getting the most *expensive* single cigar you can afford. Humidors crafted of pure cedar make a lovely stand-alone gift in lieu of the cigars themselves and can be found for under $30 at many specialty stores. If you choose to fill a humidor with cigars as a presentation tool, it's acceptable to go with the *less expensive* ones. Cigars are not stigmatized like cigarettes. In fact, cigars are widely considered distinguished and classy . . . even by nonsmokers.

Moderate

For those who have to wear them, neckties are always a fabulous gift, and those who don't will still inevitably need one for that obligatory wedding or funeral. You can easily spend $250 for a necktie from a high-end designer; however, there are plenty of great ties in the $85 range. Each brand has its own personality, so you'll need to invest a little time browsing until one leaps out at you and speaks the name of the person for whom you're shopping. For this particular personality type, I'd stay away from pastels and crazy prints. Less is more with the *mature traditional* man. If he travels, an elegant leather necktie case will protect his ties from wrinkling. For an added touch of class, engrave the giftee's initials on the case. You can give the tie and the traveling case together as one unit or as separate gifts for two different occasions.

Expensive

Help him relieve stress and stay in shape with a punching bag and boxing gloves. The punching bag itself should run you about $200 (with installation), and high-quality boxing gloves are about $100. Even if he doesn't have a workout room in his house, and most of us don't, this is a fun addition to the garage or even a home office. You can add a jump rope and boxing trunks to the gift set, or save them as presents for the next holiday.

Lavish

If you're Russell Crowe or Tom Cruise, having your own punching bag in your home gym isn't enough. So take your cue from these box-office giants the next time you're on the road. While filming *Gladiator*, the studio provided Russell with his very own mobile gym. These fully equipped luxury trailers rent for $4,000 per week and house state-of-the-art equipment and amenities. It was driven down to Mexico, where the movie was being filmed, and parked on the set with twenty-four-hour access.

FOR WOMEN

Personal Gifts
[for Birthday/Christmas/Hanukkah/Mother's Day]

Inexpensive

Cozy fuzzy slippers will be appreciated year-round. There's nothing better than sliding your feet into a yummy pair of slippers on those chilly mornings or when you're lounging around the house on those lazy weekends. Whether they're paired with a robe, pajamas or sweatpants, the *mature traditional* woman will find many opportunities to wear them. Make sure they're made of a material that is machine washable whenever possible. Open-toed, open-backed slippers are great for summer; closed styles (especially the super-fuzzy ones) are ideal for winter. Color is wide open here since they won't have to be matched to an outfit. Be sure to make a note of the color you choose, as a coordinated robe or set of pajamas will make a great follow-up gift down the road.

Moderate

Natalie Maines of the legendary Dixie Chicks once told me, "You can never have too many purses . . . cuz they always fit." Truer words have never been spoken. The *mature traditional* female will surely already have a great basic handbag (and if she doesn't, that would make a great *expensive* gift for her), so go with purses she can use for special events and social outings. Whether a wristlet or a clutch, choose something that's unusual and unlike anything she already owns. Believe me, women will find the perfect occasion to sport a new handbag. *Traditional* women will love purses that have been personalized in some way, especially with photos. There are a few purse manufacturers who can place a scanned image onto any style you select. Whether a sentimental mom or doting girlfriend, she'll be as excited over her photo purse as Ashanti and Alicia Keys were when we gifted them. Ashanti loved the photo bag we gave her at the BET Awards so much, she wore it on the red carpet at the following month's Radio Music Awards.

Expensive

It's the reliable "standby gift" that never disappoints: a luxurious bathrobe accompanied by bath and body products. The robes we used as gifts for *The Ellen De-Generes Show* during its inaugural month on the air are actually just under $100, leaving some room in your budget for nice lotions and/or bath oils. These are the same robes used by the famous Bellagio Hotel in Las Vegas. Fans of *Desperate Housewives* might have noticed Teri Hatcher modeling the "ultimate" robe, which we have used for many other celebrity clients. It is made of a microchenille that she'll never want to take off and retails for about $125. Trust me, it's worth every penny. And if you want to really splurge, cashmere robes are a decadent delight for the recipient. However, they will set you back at least $300.

FOR HOME

Housewarming/Host(ess)

Inexpensive

There are few things more appropriate to bring to a dinner party than a cookbook. If someone has gone to the trouble of preparing a dinner for guests, they will surely appreciate having more menu selections for their next culinary adventure. Inspire the chef! And nothing fills the shelves, counters or cabinets of a new home like beautiful cookbooks. Seek out cookbooks that include great photography of the finished dishes. With so many options, the chances of duplicating something they already have are fairly low. If in doubt or if you know the recipient already owns numerous cookbooks, stick to new releases. As with any book, I reiterate my recommendation to write a personal inscription on the inside front cover. I've received numerous cookbooks as gifts and love them all.

Moderate

Even if you aren't lucky enough to have a husband who loves to barbecue, a great barbecue set is a wonderful addition to any home. We've sold quite a few sets that come in a nice wicker or canvas storage case. For as little as $70, you can pick up a complete set that includes a rattan case, chef's hat, spatula, barbecue knife, brush, tongs, fork, apron and mitt.

Another "set" that makes a lovely housewarming/host(ess) gift is a martini set, complete with two glasses, tongs, jigger, shaker, bottle stoppers, corkscrew and stirrer. These usually come in a leather case, but other materials can make an equally impressive presentation. Throw in a respected bottle of vodka and your gift is complete.

Expensive

Who wouldn't enjoy the luxury of spending a lazy afternoon in the comfort of their own backyard? For under $300, you can acquire a hammock essentials package, which includes hammock, stand, pillow and pad. Most pads are reversible, so you'll get two style options for the price of one. If the recipient doesn't have a backyard, there are folding travel hammocks for right around $100 that are perfect for a day at the beach or for a weekend camping trip.

A variation that also makes a fabulous house-warming present is the self-inflating air mattress. It folds down to the size of a beachball and is ideal for weekend guests or the kids' slumber parties. Be sure to get the kind with the electric pump that inflates the mattress without the need for huffing, puffing or blow-dryers.

FOR BABY

Baby/Baby Shower Gifts

Inexpensive

Dealing with diapers is perhaps the least enjoyable part of parenthood. But for under $25 you can provide the new parents with unsurpassed odor and germ protection with a diaper genie. These diaper disposal systems allow for used diapers to be individually wrapped in a multibarrier film, and the standard size holds approximately thirty diapers.

Moderate

Burp cloths are best to have in large quantities, as they are perpetually dirty by their very nature. I recently found a line of burp cloths on the Internet that had an interesting shape—they were designed to fit the contour of the shoulder in order to reduce bunching and creasing. This is a great example of how you can find innovative design details that make a basic gift more alluring. Any baby store or online boutique will have countless options, ranging from high fashion to whimsical disposables.

Expensive

With babies come toys . . . lots and lots of toys. A beautiful wooden toy chest will be a lovely piece of furniture and an organizational tool for the nursery. Make sure it's fun and colorful so that it will work with multiple decorating motifs. And once the baby is grown, the toy chest can easily be repainted and converted to a sweater chest. Or, like my mother, parents might choose to preserve it as a toy chest throughout the decades for visiting nieces, nephews and grandchildren.

chapter nine

mature/
trendy/
close

Specialty stores will become your best ally when shopping for the *mature trendy* individual. This personality type really gravitates toward practicality with a modern twist. Specialty boutiques offer a broad range of colors, styles and designs, so you'll be able to go from basic to extraordinary with convenience and ease. Don't be afraid to give them a variation of something they already have, so long as it's a new arrival, part of the new season's collection or just plain fabulous.

FOR MEN

Personal Gifts
[for Birthday/Christmas/Hanukkah/Father's Day]

Inexpensive

Poker caddies and poker chip cases are great to have on hand whether he happens to partake in monthly card games with the boys or not. The dark wood caddies simply look nice on a game shelf or as a party favor. Not a poker player? Modify this fun theme by giving him poker chips made of chocolate, which are available at many specialty chocolate stores. Decks of cards and/or card dispensers are suitable substitutes or supplements.

Moderate

Whether he has already climbed aboard the grooming bandwagon or needs to be drafted, he'll be well served with a hair trimmer. This is the type of item many *mature* men are embarrassed to purchase for themselves but won't mind using in the privacy of their own bathrooms. You'll have the added benefit of being a beneficiary of their aesthetic improvement. Depending on the man's hirsute factor, there are a few different options, some of which will bump you up to the *moderate* or *expensive* category. Battery-operated "personal touch" hair trimmers are definitely *inexpensive* and perfect for "spot treatments" and quick fixes. Nose-hair trimmers are also *inexpensive*, and their specific design and purpose make them a great gift. Don't be fearful of offending the recipient in question; as long as you are indeed *close* to the person, it's perfectly appropriate and your civic duty! Beard trimmers are usually *moderately* priced, but a man with a mustache will already have one . . . so unless you're replacing or upgrading, beware. Travel grooming kits are *inexpensively* to *moderately* priced and typically include a hair trimming device of some kind, tweezers, scissors and nail clippers.

Expensive

A briefcase is (or can be) to men what purses are to women. So allow him to explore his options and realize that one briefcase is simply not enough. If he has black, get him brown. If he has formal, add a casual look to his collection. If he has an attaché style, incorporate a portfolio or flap design. Carefully assess his personal style before making your purchase. You can't go wrong with any of the following: Louis Vuitton for flashy sophistication, Zero Halliburton for the avant-garde James Bond profile, T. Anthony for masculine and elegant simplicity.

Romantic Gifts
[for Valentine's Day/Anniversary]

Inexpensive

I'll never understand how men survive without "man-bags." That notwithstanding, men's penchant for pockets full of "stuff" will be mitigated by a money clip to at least keep their cash organized. As with any gift, something that reflects the interests and personality of the recipient will make this "basic" present stand out. For example, I recently received a money clip that was inscribed with my personal and professional motto, "Carpe diem." An *inexpensive* token gift instantly became a special and treasured keepsake. So whether it's the emblem of their favorite football team, their college insignia or their astrological sign, add a personalized element to make your present both useful and thoughtful. Billfolds and travel wallets are also nice gifts, but they will probably move you up to the *moderate* price range.

Moderate

You don't have to be a bird watcher to appreciate a pair of binoculars. They're great for everything from sporting events to concerts. I recommend the compact styles as gifts because they are easy to transport and less expensive. You can turn this *moderate* gift into an *expensive* one by upgrading to night-vision binoculars (perfect for an *Alias* or *24* fan) or—one of the coolest inventions of all time—binoculars with a built-in digital camera ($200–$400+). Not only will these camera binoculars allow him to capture digital images and video as seen through the binocular lens, he'll also be able to download the images to his computer quite easily via a USB connection.

Expensive

Massage chairs can be pricey (anywhere from $500 to $3,000) and are available at practically every shopping mall. But consider this a gift for yourself as well as your man and consequently divide the price by two! It takes relaxing in front of the television to a whole new level. If the massage chair he wants is totally out of your budget, settle for a handheld massager, a footrest massager or even a gift certificate for a massage.

Lavish

We turned this *expensive* gift into a *lavish* one when shopping for Sarah Michelle Gellar and Jack Black a few years ago. They were hosting the MTV Movie Awards, and the network wanted to get them something extra-special. We ultimately went with $5,000 super-deluxe black leather massage chairs, which were apparently quite the hit with both Sarah and Jack.

FOR WOMEN

Personal Gifts
[for Birthday/Christmas/Hanukkah/Mother's Day]

Inexpensive

Whether it's yoga, gardening, cycling, running or horseback riding, you'll have dozens of options in accessorizing her hobby. The item will be used often and has a high "thoughtfulness quotient." Additionally, the focus is on the activity as opposed to the gift itself, so the price tag is secondary. Although the list is nearly limitless, here are a few examples to get you started: For spin class junkies, consider cute spin socks. For gardeners, a new pair of colorful gloves will add flair to her pastime. Yoga enthusiasts will love a new yoga mat. Pick up a pedometer for runners, joggers or power walkers. Buy your favorite chef a new set of spatulas. Purchase a sketch pad for the artist in your life.

Moderate

Chenille throws have become quite affordable and are the perfect accent for a chaise, sofa or even bed. Retailers such as Pottery Barn and Pier 1 often have the full spectrum of colors at a very *moderate* price point. You'll have many options in terms of both prints and finishings; my personal recommendation is a solid color with a tasseled fringe. Choose something that will complement their color scheme without needing to exactly match. Lighter and more subtle is often best when it comes to guessing about colors in home furnishing accents such as a throw. So go with beige as opposed to chocolate, mauve instead of red and peach rather than orange. Of course, if you are familiar with their home, you'll have carte blanche in selecting any color that works best. Throws are available in other elegant fabrics, such as velvet and cashmere, so explore accordingly.

Expensive

Scarves emanate a European sophistication and stylishness that speak to the *mature trendy* woman. I like to go whimsical and fun when giving scarves, so she'll have an unusual alternative to her Hermès (or Hermès-like) standards. I once gifted actress Lauren Holly with a hand-knit lavender scarf with eyelash threads. She loved it so much that she integrated it into her wardrobe for the filming of a subsequent made-for-TV movie called *Caught in the Act*. Nice scarves are expensive (at least $100), so if you're going with this particular gift suggestion, make sure you err on the side of quality. It's better to choose a different item altogether than to go cheap.

Romantic Gifts
[for Valentine's Day/Anniversary]

Inexpensive

Whatever her reading interests, you'll titillate with a magazine subscription. It's a gift that will provide ongoing entertainment. Whether she's a soap opera addict, political savant or architecture buff, there's something for everyone in the wonderful world of publishing. Most magazines offer both six- and twelve-month subscription options, so depending on the cover price, you'll be able to stay within your budget. It's always a nice idea to pick up an actual copy at the newsstand and attach a note saying she'll be receiving weekly or monthly issues in honor of the special day. Many credit cards offer points toward magazine subscriptions as a usage bonus, so you might be able to score the gift without even going out of pocket.

Moderate

Serving trays come in wicker, wood, aluminum and plastic and can cost as little as $15. You can either get a flat tray and then simply buy the supplemental "in bed" serving stand, or purchase one that comes with fold-down legs already attached for this purpose. You'll need to add the thoughtful, romantic gesture for the more substantial part of this gift. By now you've surely noticed the recurring theme that the true value of most gifts doesn't need to be the cash spent. The real worth comes from putting some effort and personal time into the implementation. So serve her breakfast in bed. Add a single rose in a bud vase, a nice cloth napkin and fresh-squeezed orange juice to your presentation, and she'll feel like a queen.

Of course, there are more *expensive* trays that incorporate antique picture frames, French tapestry fabrics, teak wood and other exquisite details. They can be used for serving food, as candle displays on coffee tables or for centerpieces on a dining room table. Whatever the end use, these trays will provide an element of hospitality, charm and elegance to her home.

Expensive

Whether she travels for work or for pleasure, having a talking electronic translator is as useful as it is original. The models get better and better each year, but for $200, current pocket-size translation devices offer 180,000 words and 20,000 phrases in nine different languages: English, German, French, Spanish, Italian, Chinese, Japanese, Korean and Russian. Unlike a dictionary, it even pronounces the words for you. This is the type of gift everyone will want to borrow.

FOR HOME

Housewarming/Host(ess) Gifts

Inexpensive

With front doors, back doors, garage doors and side doors, another doormat will always come in handy.

Earth tones are best in terms of camouflaging dirt and mud. As for design, something simple like "Welcome" or a hospitality pineapple will do the trick. As usual, any specific information you have about interests and family personality will allow you to customize. Add an international touch based on their heritage by saying "welcome" in a foreign language. The following doormats are widely available: *Bienvenidos* (Spanish), *Bienvenu* (French), *Benvenuti* (Italian) or *Wilkommen* (German). Although I discourage getting the ones with the family's last name on it, if you do, please remember that there is no apostrophe in "The Wests" or "The Farys"—it's simply plural, not possessive.

Moderate

Having a great stash of assorted board games is useful for ongoing entertainment needs. Whether providing a distraction for kids on a rainy afternoon or offering the perfect backdrop for a group gathering of competitive friends, the gift of assorted board games will likely be used on more than one occasion by your host. From Trivial Pursuit to Twister and checkers to backgammon, the options abound. This is also a great present to bring to a dinner party if your hosts have children . . . things like age-appropriate games, coloring books, puzzles and sketch pads will help keep the kids occupied while the adults socialize.

I've often used board games and cards to create a get-well gift basket. You can add magazines, handheld electronic gaming units and other distractions to help the person more actively pass their recuperation time.

Expensive

Once you've experienced the benefit of having an air filter in your home, you'll want to share the gift with your friends and loved ones at the first appropriate occasion. Although the better-quality room filters are typically $399 and up, you can find desktop models for $150–$199 and personal travel units for as little as $50.

Take this gift idea from *expensive* to *inexpensive* by visiting the aisle at your grocery store with the room deodorizes and plug-in scent dispensers. These units aren't air filters, but they're a super-affordable alternative with some similar perceived benefits. It may not make the air healthier, but it will make the room smell nicer. Be environmentally conscious when possible by choosing nonaerosols.

FOR BABY

Baby/Baby Shower Gifts

Inexpensive

Toxic cleaning products pose both immediate and long-term health risks. Because they're such a mundane commodity, cleaners often get overlooked by otherwise conscientious parents. So purchase the new parents a set of nontoxic, biodegradable, environmentally friendly cleaning products. From glass cleaner to dishwashing liquid, there are safe alternatives that are readily available at many major grocery chains and drugstores. Package them in a cute bucket or tub and you've got a clever and useful gift.

Moderate

Allowing kids to express their artistic side without ruining the good tablecloths and place mats (and walls, for that matter) can be a challenge . . . but not with "doodle mats" and "doodle tablecloths." They come with water-based markers that can simply be wiped clean at the end of a meal or sitting.

Expensive

Most new parents take immediate steps to baby-proof their home in some of the more obvious ways (outlets, toilets, cabinets). Remove all of the doubt and concern by hiring a baby-proofing service to come in and completely refit the new parents' home. This will definitely appeal to the protectively doting nature of *mature* moms and dads. Professionals will always be able to find all possible problem areas and catch some of the more obscure dangers that might go undetected by the untrained eye.

chapter ten

mature/
trendy/
casual

The *mature trendy* individual with whom you have a *casual* relationship represents that fine line between pushing the envelope and settling for a more conservative gift. Their *maturity* restrains their *trendiness*, while their *trendy* nature creates a more free-spirited *maturity*. It's an interesting balance that is further complicated by the fact that you may not know them well enough to select the most appropriate means of recognizing their frivolity while still respecting their sense of what's familiar. Any "research" you might be able to easily obtain will serve you well. In the absence of any Nancy Drew abilities, I recommend taking the high road of caution with functional gifts that boast an innovative or creative touch.

FOR MEN

Personal Gifts
[for Birthday/Christmas/Hanukkah/Father's Day]

Inexpensive

Ever forget to buy a gift for a particular occasion? As a result, you probably had to stop at a 7-Eleven on your way to the party and pick up a bottle of liquor (in order to fully demonstrate your forgetfulness). Surprisingly, convenience stores offer one of the most original birthday gifts I've ever received: lottery tickets in a quantity to match the birthday being celebrated. You can also select a random quantity or the number of years you've known the person. This is a very versatile idea and can even be used as a baby gift; simply attach a note that says "I hope this will result in the start of Little Johnny's trust fund."

Moderate

Men tend to accumulate watches, cuff links and assorted jewelry over the years and need to keep them organized and protected from scratching. Watch boxes, bureau valets and pocket changers are usually made of either wood or leather and are a great way to reduce clutter. Many models are perfect catchalls for keys, cell phones, change, receipts, cash and, of course, jewelry and watches. For a touch of personalization, add an engraved brass plaque to the front of the valet.

Expensive

Every man needs nice cuff links for formal and business events. Cuff links should be a conversation piece whenever possible, so look for semiprecious stones and chunky metals that reflect the personality of the man receiving them. Favorite colors, hobbies and birthstones are a good place to start. If he only wears French cuffs with his tuxedo, you'll want to stick with understated elegance. If he is stylish enough to wear French cuffs with his business suits, you'll be able to have more fun and explore more dramatic options. Gold or silver is a personal preference, but in general you'll want to match the tone of his watch(es) and/or wedding band. And it's always nice to have both options when getting ready, so now you have two fabulous gifts to give him!

FOR WOMEN

Personal Gifts
[for Birthday/Christmas/Hanukkah/Mother's Day]

Inexpensive

Whether it's rainy or snowy, having a stylish umbrella will make the day seem less gloomy. Bright solid colors, understated houndstooth or feminine pastel prints are all fantastic options, since most people's current umbrella is either black or a promotional item with a big company logo on it. One of my favorite umbrellas is something I bought while in Italy. When opened, the underside of the umbrella reveals a reproduction of Michelangelo's *The Creation* from the Sistine Chapel. Small sizes will be relatively *inexpensive*, while the larger umbrellas can slip into the *moderate* price range. Many retail clothing chains offer attractive and affordable styles. You'll never go wrong with a mini black travel umbrella that can be stashed in a suitcase so that the recipient will always be prepared for inclement weather.

You can expand this "rainy day" theme with fun and colorful rubber boots, galoshes or even a waterproof parka.

Moderate

There is plenty of research that has led to the development of many vitamins and supplements specifically designed for women's unique needs. These products are available at any health food or vitamin store and range from multivitamins to calcium supplements. The *mature* woman is often too selfless to focus on her own needs, so assemble a starter set for her. Have the store's on-site expert assist you with recommendations on brands and product lines.

Expensive

The *mature* woman is likely to have a clearly established preference in her musical taste. Whatever her favorite band/group/singer/performer, you'll be hitting a home run by giving her tickets to a local concert or performance. Two tickets will suffice, and it's totally okay if the performance date is a few weeks or even months away. If you plan far enough ahead, you can write to the group's publicist and get an autographed picture to include with the tickets for a little extra sizzle. When my very resourceful friend JL took me to a Barbra Streisand event for my birthday, she included the tickets with a framed photograph of Barbra and me . . . an intimate photo that had been computer-engineered by placing my head on Dustin Hoffman's body.

FOR HOME

Housewarming/Host(ess) Gifts

Inexpensive

Ever needed a flashlight and couldn't quite remember in which drawer or cabinet it was placed? I certainly have. And that's precisely why a flashlight (with a pack of appropriate batteries) makes the perfect housewarming gift. For a slightly higher price, many camping and hardware stores offer "emergency flashlights" as well; these can be hand-cranked or recharged by solar power. The flashlight is less appropriate as a host(ess) gift, so my adaptation for that occasion is to pick up several packs of those amazingly handy utility lighters. They conveniently remove the need for annoying matches when lighting fires and candles.

Along the lines of household must-haves, stepladders and space heaters also make ideal housewarming gifts. In fact, a space heater is a superb present for any woman for any occasion, especially if she's perpetually cold, like the women in my life. No office or home can ever be kept too warm for most women, so she'll appreciate the extra warmth no matter where she uses the heater.

Moderate

Most home accessory stores carry stylish storage boxes. These are usually made of rattan or leather, come with a lid or handles, are stackable and look amazing on bookshelves or under coffee tables. Everyone has stuff that they'd love to have within arm's reach if only it looked more presentable. Well, now you can help make that dream a reality. You'll enable them to elegantly store everything from receipts and photos to CDs and magazines.

Expensive

Having a beautiful wreath on the door is one of those touches that makes a house feel like a home. But it's not always at the top of the list of necessary acquisitions by the *mature* and sensible home owner. So whether it's a fresh mulberry or holly wreath for the holidays or dried roses and magnolia, your gift will provide a seasonal decorating element that may have otherwise gone unfulfilled. There are numerous mail-order catalogs that offer beautiful options. If you send it early enough (i.e., early December), this also makes a lovely Christmas gift that can be enjoyed throughout the holiday season.

FOR BABY

Baby/Baby Shower Gifts

Inexpensive

Although there's not an actual price tag, offering someone your babysitting services is a priceless gift. In this day and age, parents who have someone they trust to watch their children receive peace of mind in addition to a much-needed break from their parental obligations. I really like giving my time as a formalized gift (and even make a corresponding gift certificate for the services being offered), because it makes it more comfortable for the parents to request the favor . . . a favor for which they may otherwise feel too awkward or guilty to ask. This way, they'll be able to ask you to sacrifice your personal plans on a Saturday night without any pangs of guilt whatsoever!

Moderate

Baby jewelry is perhaps an accessory more appreciated by parents and onlookers than the baby itself. Nevertheless, sentimental and/or personalized baby jewelry is a great way to go for *mature trendy* parents. One year at the GRAMMYs, we created a set of three charm bracelets for Faith Hill, each spelling out in block letters the name of one of her three beautiful daughters: Audrey, Maggie and Gracie. The bracelets were sterling silver with pink accents (one of Faith's favorite colors). On another occasion we were commissioned to create mother-daughter anklets as a gift from an agent to one of her celebrity clients. The matching set was not only exquisite but a nice means of facilitating "fashion bonding" between mother and daughter. The set we created was made of jade with gold finishings. Because of the unpredictable growth of infants, the baby's version was on an expandable elastic-type band. Using the baby's birthstone is always a nice choice but in no way mandatory.

Expensive

Vintage 1930s tricycles, in blue or pink, are collectible, decorative and useable. Besides having an amazing aesthetic, it's the type of "toy" that can be passed down for generations since it just becomes cooler and cooler with age. These tricycles will look as great in the nursery as they do in the garage (or driveway). No matter where it's stored, this gift will certainly elicit oohs and ahhs from the recipient.

Lavish

Starting at around $8,000, custom-made tree houses are enjoyed by many celebrities' children. The themes range from fortresses and castles to boats and spaceships, with amenities like balconies, slides and trap doors. Industrious parents who have some basic carpentry and artistic abilities can create this amazing resource for their kids without hiring an *expensive* architect or designer. For the rest of us, we'll just have to slip into a celebrity backyard.

chapter eleven

my
favorite
things

Since I'm reputed to be hard to buy for (a common complaint among gift shoppers), I thought I'd share a few of the best gifts I've ever received. These are in no particular order; they simply stand out in my mind as some of my favorites over the years. Perhaps one of them will provide the inspiration you need to please that "discerning" person on your gift list:

1. *Any* type of candle (especially large pillars and round three-wicks, but even tea lights and votives have been wonderfully useful).

2. Chocolate brown glacé leather briefcase.

3. Boots from my favorite shoe designer.

4. An industrial mixer—which has made my baking adventures even more enjoyable.

5. Large potted orchids.

6. Many, many cookbooks—my all-time favorite was given to me over ten years ago: *Best of America* from the American Family Cooking Library . . . if I could keep only one cookbook, this would be it.

7. A Belgian waffle maker—which allows me to make the most amazingly easy yet impressive breakfast for guests.

8. Portable DVD player.

9. Clothing (or a gift certificate) from my favorite clothing boutique.

10. The picture frames that fill my home.

11. A set of high-quality chef's knives that changed my culinary life. (Follow-up Gift Alert: If they like great knives, they'll *love* an electric knife sharpener to maintain your wonderful original gift.)

12. A bottle of Barbra Streisand Collector's Reserve limited-edition wine.

13. Surprise bouquets of fresh flowers—especially on all those days when it *wasn't* my birthday!

14. DVDs of my favorite movies and TV shows.

15. Fun T-shirts to wear to the gym.
16. Leopard coasters.
17. High-thread-count bed linens and pillowcases—queen size in cream or beige if you're ever sending me a gift!
18. Jewelry—ranging from leather cuffs and silver rings to turquoise necklaces and vintage cuff links.
19. Diamond watch—rose-colored face with tan ostrich leather band.
20. Beautiful note cards and stationery.
21. Self-cleaning electric razor.
22. Colorful bamboo bowls with matching place mats.
23. Rock 'n' roll chunky silver keychain in the form of a gothic "L."
24. TiVo. (FYI: It will change the way they watch TV!)
25. Set of large coffee mugs reflective of the grape theme in my kitchen.
26. A glass paperweight with an etched engraving of the main lyric from Barbra Streisand's hit song "People."
27. Cashmere socks.
28. CD from an artist the giver "thought I would love" (which is how I discovered one of my now-favorite singers, Eva Cassidy).

29. Sheet music of my favorite pop ballads.
30. An annual collector's series Christmas ornament whose subject matter has both personal and historical significance.

You'll notice that some of these items were *expensive*, yet many were not. Some were predictably based on my *young/trendy* personality profile, yet others spoke to the *mature* or *traditional* facets of my character. But each gift was related to an express interest or personal passion . . . making it a perfect present!

chapter twelve

group gifts

Certain events call for giving a group or bulk gift rather than one that epitomizes individuality: namely, dinner parties, weddings and wedding-related activities such as bachelor(ette) parties. In my experience, the gift options for these situations are dictated by budget and are meant to be a mere token or remembrance rather than a pricey present. Even at celebrity weddings, for instance, the gifts for guests tend to be quite modest. Classy, elegant and thematic . . . but not particularly expensive. However, the perception of the present needs to be substantial enough that the item will be kept and not discarded immediately.

Weddings

The general rule of thumb at weddings is that the guests are already being treated to a (presumably) nice meal and party. The ideal "guest gift" at your wedding is one that makes a nice memento while simultaneously enhancing the place setting. You'll also want to make sure that the size of the item doesn't detract from the table décor. Whatever gift you choose, I always recommend attaching a small note card of some sort to each one, thanking the guests for attending your event and letting them know that the particular item is a present to be taken home. Here are my ten favorite choices from the weddings I've done:

- Miniature picture frames with crystal adornments that complement the color scheme of the wedding. You can use these to display either the place card, photo of the bride and groom or, for small weddings, your favorite photograph of that specific guest.
- Jar-style candles made of colored glass, wrapped in decorative Italian paper or presented in a mini organza bag.
- Sachets filled with potpourri.

- Individually wrapped chocolates. I particularly love champagne truffles for a special occasion like a wedding. Remember that any item, regardless of its price tag, will seem much more impressive if you take the time to individually wrap it and top it off with lovely ribbon or an elegant garnish such as a flower. Any gourmet chocolatier will make individual boxes of chocolate ideal for this purpose.

- Glass, crystal or pewter bud vases with a single flower that complements the centerpiece.

- Swarovski crystal "director's chair" place card holders (that will later serve as business card holders). You can substitute any appropriately thematic object as the holder.

- Aromatherapy travel pillows or eye pillows. These are especially great when it's an out-of-town wedding.

- Message stones with inspirational or romantic words etched onto colored glass.

- Mini or individual bottles of champagne with custom labels. If your budget permits, add silver champagne straws and chocolate-dipped strawberries for truly elegant gift ensembles.

- Mini books with romantic poems or inspirational quotes.

When your wedding is taking place in a location that lends itself to a particular theme, you will be able to explore options that exceed the mere aesthetic of the table. If you marry in Hawaii, for example, you might consider using orchids, a beach-related item or a customized lei. If your big day is in Las Vegas, gambling-related merchandise or poolside accessories work perfectly. When sitcom star Leah Remini tied the knot in Vegas, each of her guests received a pool-themed gift assortment including sandals, sunglasses, lip balm, sarongs and suntan lotion. Weddings that fall on or around major holidays can take advantage of any appropriate holiday-related paraphernalia or tie-ins. For Easter, consider a Fabergé-style decorative egg. St. Patrick's Day conjures up notions of glass bottles filled with green mint bath or massage oil. A pumpkin spice quick bread or latte mix presented in a gourd is perfect for a Thanksgiving wedding. And Mardi Gras provides the wonderfully flamboyant opportunity to incorporate masks made of feathers, sequins and glitter.

Unless you're a celebrity or having a very small wedding, particularly one where people traveled a great distance to attend, I discourage the use of gift bags for attendees. They are very difficult to produce well (at least on a budget) and require much more work than you'd expect. Trust me on this one. You'll get much more bang for your buck by focusing on a single guest gift that doubles as a table decoration or accent. It's always better to do a simple gift *well* than to fall short when striving for a grander gesture.

When gifting your bridesmaids and groomsmen at a wedding, tradition will help keep you focused. The generally accepted custom of giving members of your wedding party something they can actually wear during the ceremony (and beyond) is one that I support. I believe in embracing tradition when it's plainly good gifting advice! All of the gifts should be identical or comparable; the maid/matron/man of honor and the best man might receive slight upgrades of the same present.

For the ladies, a respectable piece of jewelry does the trick: necklaces, bracelets, rings, hair clips or even toe rings . . . anything that complements their dresses and makes the statement you want at your wedding. Since girls love beauty products, you can also fill a monogrammed toiletry bag or travel tote with lotions, creams, cosmetics and fragrances. This "beauty bag" concept makes a great gift for any number of occasions where girlfriends are gathering, ranging from wedding showers to slumber parties. If you have room in your budget, include a fabulous pair of comfy pajamas or a sexy negligé.

For the men, cuff links, watches, cigars, tie clips, money clips, wallets or luxury pens are always well received. A nice bottle of wine or champagne is a great gift for groomsmen, especially if you have a custom label made commemorating the event or package it with a leather or wooden tote and deluxe wine opener (see Chapter Four). Alcohol also makes a great gift for bachelor parties. Add a bottle of distinctive vodka to a martini shaker, martini glasses, jar of imported olives and bartender's handbook for the ultimate "Bachelor's Martini Madness" set. Although the bachelor party by nature tends to err on the side of tackiness and inappropriateness, the gentlemen's gift bags can creatively and tastefully celebrate the occasion. Modified "hangover kits" (see Chapter Five) work well for these types of festivities; you can customize based on the location of the soirée and the proclivities of the attendees.

Dinner Parties

Although it's in no way required or expected, you may choose to provide your dinner guests with a parting gift. If you go down this path, you'll want to stick to presents that work well with the theme of the cuisine you are serving, complement your home or kitchen décor, or relate in some way to the reason for the gathering. In addition to the above-referenced suggestions for weddings (which work equally well here . . . and vice versa), the following are nice touches for a dinner party:

- Small decorative bottle of olive oil, dipping oil or imported vinegar.
- Beautiful box of matches—the type you'd place by your hearth.
- Mini basket with gingham napkin and a fresh-baked muffin for breakfast the next morning.
- Individually wrapped fresh flower. A long-stem rose or Casablanca lily works great for this purpose—simply have the florist wrap it in clear plastic with a piece of raffia string.
- Mini "good night" beauty kit with eye gel, nighttime moisturizer, mask and toner.
- A CD you've burned of the mood music you played that evening. Put the date and the names of the guests on the CD label.
- Canister or bag of the tea or coffee you served.
- Little three-ring binder with the recipes for the dishes you served.
- Gourmet oversized iced fortune cookie with a customized fortune placed inside.

There are certainly less common occasions, such as reunions, conventions and special events. Although they are not addressed here, you can adapt some or all of the suggestions I've made for weddings and dinner parties. Generally speaking, seek out inexpensive items that enhance the theme or nature of the event. There are usually obvious tie-ins and associations that can be dressed up or personalized. Sometimes, you may want to take "the road less traveled" by using humor or parody for an unexpected twist. The smaller your budget, the more you'll need to rely on nostalgia and creativity. With a little time and ingenuity, you will be able to conceive of gift items that would make Martha Stewart proud. But any masterpiece begins with the seed of inspiration. Sit down with a pad of paper and brainstorm. Flip through magazines and modify some of the extravagant layouts you'll find there. Watch home-and-garden television shows and "borrow" some of their professionals' wonderful ideas. Give your gift with the knowledge and belief that it is fabulous . . . and that's just what people will perceive! As in all areas of life, confidence is contagious.

chapter thirteen

gifts
at the
office

I've done a lot of corporate gifts over the years for law firms, realtors, talent agencies, studios and even NASCAR. Some have been group gifts, while others were completely individualized; they've ranged from knickknacks to high-end electronics. I've noticed a few consistent themes in how companies approach stellar gifting, as well as common mistakes I see made time and time again. Whether you're the owner of the company, the supervisor of a department, the office manager or the executive assistant tasked with doing your boss' shopping, here are some basic guidelines to keep in mind.

Do

- Do give a gift of some sort to all employees during the holidays and for birthdays.
- Do give gifts to your boss (assuming you like your job and would like to keep it).
- Do give gifts to any client with whom you'd like to continue doing business.
- Do include a personalized note with each present whenever possible. I know this is a lot more work than simply inserting a standard message with each gift, especially if you are buying for a large number of employees or clients. But it's worth the extra effort for reasonable quantities.
- Do order a few extra items in case you forgot someone, add last-minute staff members or have a temp who happens to be working the day you have your gift exchange.
- Do order early. When ordering large quantities and customizing in any way, you can easily double the cost of the gift with rush charges and expedited shipping. You can usually negotiate a slight discount with the vendor if you order off-peak as well. Ordering early will also allow you to mail in a check for your purchase; paying cash (i.e., a non-credit-card

transaction) can sometimes result in a further 1% to 2% discount if you ask.

- Do give gifts that offer an "escape" from the workplace . . . something that will foster recreation or relaxation.
- Do have customized labels made for wine, champagne and similar items (it's remarkably inexpensive).

Don't

- Don't give racy or sexual gifts. You need to cater to the lowest common denominator in terms of how easily someone might be offended. You certainly wouldn't want a gift intended as a joke to lead to a sexual harassment lawsuit. In this day and age, you simply cannot be too careful.
- Don't include your company name or logo on employee gifts. They know where they work. If you include it on client gifts for marketing reasons, make it discreet and subtle. For example, if giving a bathrobe, use tone-on-tone embroidery; when giving a leather product, emboss it on the inside rather than outside.
- Don't assume that everyone's religious affiliation is the same as yours.

- Don't give clients exceedingly lavish gifts . . . it actually may be perceived as a bribe and make them uncomfortable. This also applies to your boss—you want to win brownie points but not come off as trying too hard.

With that said, there are four classifications of people to whom gifts are typically given in the workplace:

- Coworkers
- Subordinates
- Superiors
- Clients

For the most part, you'll use the same process laid out in Chapter One to determine the type of person you're gifting and proceed accordingly. Many of the same gift ideas I've already suggested will be equally successful in the workplace.

Coworkers

As a group, your office community should decide whether you want to celebrate all employee birthdays or none. This situation should be honestly assessed to avoid intra-office strife, where people feel compelled to participate in a group gifting environment out of peer pressure. Gifting should be a loving event that stems from genuine desire, not obligation. For the holidays, the Secret Santa approach is an effective means of celebrating the occasion without creating an undue financial burden on staff members, since each person only needs to buy one gift. Many offices choose to bring in a present or toy for an employee-chosen children's charity in lieu of gifts for one another.

If you do decide to celebrate in some way, whatever the occasion, you'll want to treat everyone consistently across the board. For birthdays, I recommend keeping it simple and inexpensive; you might have a fresh bagel breakfast each time or a cake from a local bakery. People are more likely to appreciate their contribution if they also get something out of it, like breakfast. Another option is to establish a standard donation that everyone contributes toward a gift card from Barnes & Noble, Starbucks or a local movie theater. Or simply have your entire department sign a birthday card and get together for an afternoon coffee break. Acknowledgment and a little camaraderie are lovely gifts in and of themselves.

If you are friends with particular colleagues outside of work, I recommend keeping your gifting personal and not making it part of the office environment. It's amazing how easily people's feelings can be hurt when they feel excluded. The point of a gift is to make others feel great, so it's always best to minimize the risk of achieving the opposite result.

Subordinates

Especially with large companies, give the same holiday present to all employees to avoid jealousy. For key employees, use tenure anniversaries to differentiate gifts. It's totally acceptable to give different but equally priced gifts to men and women. If you have a small staff, enjoy personalizing each gift as you normally would. Whatever you do, find a cost-effective way of making your staff feel special and appreciated.

Gifts don't have to come in a box, so think about offering a service as a gift to your employees . . . such as bringing in a coffee cart, an ice cream sundae bar, roaming massage therapists for the day or even a gourmet omelet station. However, *don't* give an "office party" or "office dinner" as an employee gift. Not everyone wants to be "rewarded" by hanging out with the same people they have to see every day, and they may not relish the idea of bonding with you after work hours.

If your company gives a cash bonus as its holiday gift, make sure it's presented in a creative way that will make it stand out from any other paycheck. It can be something as simple as including a personalized card where you express your gratitude for their hard work. If your business is experiencing cash-flow issues that might preclude spending money on an actual physical present, give your employees extra time off with pay. They will totally value the gesture, and you won't be out any incremental cash in your budget.

Christmas has indeed become a widely celebrated holiday in America and in many ways transcends a strictly religious connotation, but be sure to consider your Jewish employees. I've found that Jewish colleagues typically don't mind celebrating the holiday, but I do recommend being as sensitive and inclusive as possible. Think about conducting your office gift exchange during the eight days of Hanukkah. Stick to general "holiday" references as opposed to more limited "Christmas" festivities. Take the time to find out whether your staff members observe Christmas, Hanukkah, Kwanzaa or even Solstice; offer them the opportunity to express and represent all holiday customs.

Superiors

It makes good business sense to give a little something to your immediate supervisor, especially for the holidays and his or her birthday. Your superiors won't expect anything lavish, but they truthfully do expect something (whether they admit that or not). A group gift from the entire department is often the easiest way to go. And although it's a bit more burdensome, those staff members with substantially higher salaries should voluntarily contribute a little more or discreetly give a secondary gift on their own.

Clients

You want the people who spend money with you to feel valued. You also want your gift to embody the same qualities for which they have hired you: class and creativity. Even if you are simply sending out a holiday or New Year's greeting card, make sure it's something that stands out and somehow incorporates your company's personality. *Always* (there are no exceptions) handwrite a personal message on the inside of the card . . . and that means more than just signing your name! If you aren't willing to add this single personal gesture, you should just forgo sending a card altogether.

Don't use a holiday gift or card as an excuse to ignore your clients the rest of the year. You'll want to make a point of remembering key clients for special occasions throughout the year. You should always find out from your clients' assistants specific information, like their birthday, anniversary and religious affiliation. Even a simple birthday card is a wonderful gesture for an important client.

Lead by Example

Gifts in the workplace are quite important. You see many work associates more often than your friends and family. It's an environment where people's perceptions of you can be directly reflected in promotions, raises and revenue generation. Make it a personal goal to be perceived as the most thoughtful and generous person in your office. Lead by example when it comes to fabulous gift giving!

chapter fourteen

thinking
outside
the basket

The vast majority of the gifts you'll ever give will fall into one of five packaging categories: (1) a gift basket, (2) a gift bag, (3) a wrapped box, (4) a gift certificate/envelope or (5) a shipped package. I utilize all five on a regular basis and will use one over another depending on client preference, personal preference, logistical necessity or budgetary necessity (or all of the above). If you are on a limited budget, it means you'll need to give even more thought to the presentation. An inexpensive gift with amazing gift wrapping will automatically be perceived as having a greater value. Let's discuss some basic concepts for each of these packaging categories.

The Gift Basket

They are called gift baskets. People are obsessed with them. Stars love them. My company is famous for them. Most important, award show gift baskets provide a valuable lesson for those looking to spice up their gift giving: Think outside the basket!

Just say no to cellophane and wicker. This sort of mundane approach to gift baskets certainly has its place, and sometimes simply can't be avoided for expediency and budgetary reasons. But since presentation really is everything, and you only have one chance to make a first impression, make sure you spend a little time and energy investigating imaginative options. It will definitely make your gift stand out. If you do have to go the traditional route and use an actual basket, add your own personal touches. Visit a local fabric store to pick up tulle and inexpensive remnants, which will make gorgeous substitutes for cellophane. Stock up on masculine stripes and solids as well as feminine florals and prints. Have fun exploring and experimenting as you tap into your creative spirit!

Gifts within gifts have become my company's trademark. We like to use luggage for all of our award shows. Celebs simply wheel away their swag (an acronym for "sealed with a gift") in an amazing piece of luggage that they can use over and over again. But you can scale down the concept by substituting purses, backpacks, picnic baskets, flowerpots, chests, cake pans, ottomans, hampers, vases, wagons, antique boxes or nearly any other "vessel." The point is to find something the recipient will enjoy and use. It should also enhance the theme of your gift basket, which I find is the easiest way to organize any product assortment.

Themes will keep your shopping efforts focused and will also allow you to include less expensive items that would otherwise be inappropriate because of their low value. For example, you could do a "Fashionista Bag": a purse filled with fabulous beauty products and fun accessories. If you're creating a "Bachelor(ette) Gift Bag," you can have fun exploring erotic toys, lingerie and sexually explicit magazines. For a gardening buff, you might fill a large flowerpot with tulip bulbs, a small hand shovel and gloves. When giving a wedding gift, wrap the basket in a piece of white sheer fabric that is reminiscent of a bridal veil (or buy an actual veil at a costume store or thrift shop); finish it off with a grouping of small flowers resembling a bridal bouquet.

We were recently hired to create a birthday gift basket for a well-known actress celebrating her twenty-sixth birthday. Her mother told us in advance that she loved "girly things" and that her favorite color was purple. Assembling the "girly" beauty and fashion items was easy and included a purse, a bathing suit, a plush robe, high-end skin-care products, a laptop bag, a funky scarf, a cashmere sweater and many other goodies. For the presentation, we ordered a cream-colored wooden chest with hand-painted flowers. Amidst the gifts we interspersed purple orchids and lavender roses (which we had specially imprinted with her photo and "Happy 26th Birthday"). The entire ensemble was then draped and wrapped with embroidered purple fabric. It was spectacular and immensely fun to conceptualize.

The Gift Bag

This is often just a scaled-down version of a gift basket. From a business perspective, it's sometimes the only way to time-effectively handle a last-minute gift request and is certainly the most cost-effective. When used by an individual for a personal gift, it's quite frankly the easy way out. Oftentimes, people will simply throw their gift into a purchased paper gift bag out of sheer laziness. Let me share a couple of little things you can do to make this technique appear less thoughtless and more impressive.

You must include nice tissue paper that is color-coordinated with the bag. One sheet is inadequate. You should first wrap the gift itself in a piece of the tissue paper and place it in the bottom of the bag. Then take an individual sheet at its center point between the tips of your fingers and lift it up. Give it a good flick of your wrist to provide the tissue with body and shape. At this point, you should have something that loosely resembles a tubular flower. Gently stuff the pointed tip of the tissue into the bag, and repeat this process until you have placed one sheet along all sides of the item. Don't overhandle the tissue paper; one flick should be sufficient.

Once you've surrounded the object with tissue paper, you should have a gift bag with a nice flourish of tissue sticking out of the top. Write your card and add it to the mix. Any extra decorative feature you have time to include will go a long way. Whenever possible, I like to wrap ivy (fresh or faux) around the handles of the bag or simply add a flower or two to the tissue paper flourish. With a few small touches, you'll still be able to take advantage of this time-effective packaging technique while simultaneously winning points for your creative presentation.

The Wrapped Box

The majority of the gifts you'll ever give or receive in your lifetime will simply come in a wrapped box. But simple doesn't have to mean boring. So be sure to invest in beautiful wrapping paper, Scotch tape and *lots* of ribbon. You can incorporate some of the presentation ideas already mentioned to spice up your projects. Visit an arts and crafts store and stock up on accoutrements that can be added to your packages, especially silk flowers, sprigs of fruit and vines. While you're there, pick up a hot glue gun, hole punch, pipe cleaners, clear fishing line, double-sided tape, colored markers, unusual filler material and fabric scissors. Nothing can beat a hot glue gun when it comes to affixing odds and ends to your packages. The hole punch will allow you to use more original gift tags. Pipe cleaners will assist you in attaching gift tags and other accessories to your ribbon as well as in fortifying your bows. Clear fishing line is the best and strongest invisible fastener for the more uncommon items you'll soon be integrating into your presentations. And you simply can't acceptably cut most fabrics with regular scissors. I actually recommend buying at least two pairs of fabric scissors: one with a regular blade and another with a crimped edge. This will give your cut fabric a more finished and professional look.

Your all-important foundation here is to wrap the box using lovely wrapping paper. Some people are naturally talented at creating clean edges and neatly finishing off the sides. The more you do this, the better you'll get. Have you ever marveled at how perfectly and painlessly sales clerks at clothing stores can fold garments? They simply learned through repetition. The girls at my office who do our wrapping have found that using double-sided Scotch tape is a wonderful way to avoid the messiness of securing the flaps on the side of the package. Once the box is wrapped, they add the ribbon, create the bow and finish it off with some sort of fabulous garnish. Following are just a few creative ideas for those final distinctive touches.

- When giving a baby gift, attach a pair of baby booties to the bow and utilize diapers in lieu of tissue paper.
- Use rose petals instead of less attractive and less fragrant packing materials like shredded paper or tissue paper (although both are totally acceptable, especially when color-coordinated with the wrapping paper).
- During the holidays, affix sprigs of holly, fresh mistletoe or even a Christmas ornament.
- Replace a bow with fresh hydrangeas or grapes. Keep an eye out for any and all decorative elements that you can begin adding to your gift wrapping endeavors. Maintain an open mind and don't be afraid to try new and unusual things.

The Gift Certificate/Envelope

Similarly, whenever I give a gift certificate (which happens at least a dozen times for every award show we do), I always like for it to be placed in something other than a plain boring envelope. So if you're giving a gift certificate for a cooking class, attach the certificate to a whisk or other kitchen utensil with a festive ribbon. A gift certificate for a massage can be tied to one of those plastic handheld massagers. Concert tickets might be placed inside one of the artist's CDs or inside a blank CD case with a custom-printed cover that you create on your computer. The point is _not_ to buy another stand-alone present, but to simply find something super-inexpensive that matches the theme of the gift. If you hit a creative wall, balloons or a beautiful vellum envelope filled with confetti is always a safe standby. If you do use an envelope, select an unusual color, a non-standard size or an atypical material.

The Shipped Package

I'm often asked if it's still necessary to wrap a present that's being shipped. In an ideal world, you'll always beautifully wrap your gift and then have it carefully packed for shipping in order to preserve the integrity of the presentation you created. This is the scenario with which I most frequently deal on a professional level, as the majority of our gifts are sent via FedEx. However, I'll be the first to admit that this creates much more work, effort and expense. You'll need bubble wrap, packing popcorn, foam supports, shipping boxes of almost every conceivable size and plenty of shipping tape.

If you have to ship your gift, it is definitely something you should keep in the forefront of your mind when shopping. Shipping costs can double the budget for your gift if the item is large or heavy. It also means that realistically speaking it may not make as much sense to spend quite as much time on bows or other presentation elements that will likely be ruined during transit. If you know shipping will be involved, don't buy perishable or fragile items (and if you do, adequately insure the package, because if it can break it probably will). If you are shipping out of the country, keep in mind that many foreign nations have import taxes that can be costly to *the recipient*. Find out the details before shipping and investigate ways to minimize this tax.

Shipping does provide you some leeway if you're looking to avoid wrapping your gift. However, you'll still need to make some minimal creative effort. You can use brightly colored shipping popcorn mixed with wrapped candies, colored tissue paper, dried flowers and dyed foam to transform the shipping box into a gift basket of sorts.

The only time it's definitely unacceptable *not* to wrap the gift within the shipping box is for Christmas. Your gift should be able to be placed under their tree along with their other presents, which clearly requires that it be suitably prepared for that purpose. You'll also want to make the extra effort to wrap before shipping when another party will be handling your gift as an intermediary. If your present will be "passed along" for any reason, you'll want it to be wrapped with the intended recipient's name clearly written on an envelope on the outside of the package. You should also include a note to the third party with specific instructions and your personal thanks for their handling delivery on your behalf.

All of the Above

Whatever the categorization of your present, always handwrite a card or gift tag to accompany it. If you can learn a little calligraphy, that's even better. Invest $8 in a marker set so you can also color-coordinate the ink with the packaging . . . excellence is in the details!

When affixing a gift tag to any present, especially ones for casual and professional recipients, never assume that the person will know who you are based on a first name only. Make sure the gift card is not only *legible* but that you include your first and last name so that they will be able to thank you (or at the very least know who gave them the gift).

chapter fifteen

the
holidays

It's a familiar Thanksgiving scene: the turkey is golden brown and ready to be carved; the roasted chestnuts have been added to the stuffing; the fresh berry cobbler is bubbling; the table is impeccably set. What may be different, however, in *my* Thanksgiving scenario is that my holiday shopping is also complete. In fact, the gifts are even wrapped and ready to be placed under the tree. Although this feat may seem less impressive since I do own a gifting business, I want to share with you how I prepare for the mother of all gift occasions in the hopes that you'll learn to love it the way I do. It always saddens me to hear people's "bah humbug" complaints about how hectic, unenjoyable and stressful the holidays are . . . primarily because it's a completely avoidable predicament.

First and foremost, you have to get into the Christmas spirit. For me, this is easily achieved through music and holiday decorations. I begin playing Christmas music the day after Thanksgiving. My favorite holiday albums are Barbra Streisand's (both of them) and Amy Grant's (all three). I play holiday music at my home, at my office, in my car and even at the gym with the help of a "Christmas Playlist" on my iPod. The other key ingredient in establishing the proper mood is to create a festive ambiance through wreaths, candles, holiday adornments, a roaring fire and, of course, a Christmas tree. You can't help but be joyful and merry when your home is illuminated with the soft glow of firelight, the tree is beautifully decorated and candles are flickering everywhere.

Okay, now that you're in the holiday spirit, how do you tackle the seemingly insurmountable task ahead of you without undue stress? The key factor to your success is your list. After all, it has worked for Santa Claus all these years. Having a detailed gift list will keep you organized, streamlined and sane.

Have one column for giftee names, another column for your budget for each person, a column for potential gifts and two final columns to check off wrapping and delivery. Here's a sample you can use as a guide:

WRAPPED	RECIPIENT	GIFT	BUDGET	DELIVERED
✓	Bill	Gym shoes	$100	✓
	Tatiana	Jewelry	$30	
	Kathy	Ornament	$20	
✓	Mom	"I Remember" book	$300	FEDEX 12/5
	Brian & Susan	Blender/ something for new house	$50	
✓	Janet	Fashion	$50	Under tree
	Raffi	Watch for work	$250	
✓	Liz	Butterfly-related accessory for new office	$50	Office closet

On a separate sheet of paper, do a little brainstorming by thinking of everything you can associate with each person: favorite color, hobbies, interests, things they borrow from you, sizes, birthstones, children's names, favorite movies, and so on. It sounds simple and obvious, but a little advance preparation will save hours of last-minute scrambling. Take this list with you whenever you're out shopping or running errands; you'll be surprised what jumps out at you once you've learned to keep your gift needs "top of mind." Once you've purchased items, wrap them and set them aside, making sure they are clearly and securely labeled. After you ship or otherwise deliver, make an appropriate notation in the "Delivery" column of your list. If I've placed the gift in an interim location awaiting further action, I'll make a "locator" notation. Keep in mind that gift tags sometimes become detached from their packages, so for occasions where your present will be one of many, enclose your card on the inside of the box, basket, bag or other container. You'll obviously still need a recipient designation on the outside of the package as well, but this provides a little added insurance. If you're going to the trouble of giving a fabulous gift, you want to make sure you get credit for it!

This list will serve a few different purposes. Besides helping make sure no one falls through the cracks, you'll also be able to assess your budget early on. It's important to set reasonable budgets to avoid the stress of overspending. In addition, you can plan your wrapping supply needs and set aside sufficient time to implement that component. I save my lists on my computer from year to year to avoid inadvertent gift duplication. It's also easier than starting from scratch when it comes to brainstorming. If a gift was a hit the year before, I'll recycle it for those who didn't already receive it.

Just think how stressed you'd be if you decided that instead of working on that big project at the office every day for a month, you were going to wait and do the whole thing the night before. Yes, it may get done. And you may even get an "A." However, by spreading your work out (that includes shopping and wrapping), you'll not only save time and money but also enjoy the holidays a lot more. Starting in June (at the latest), create an exercise for yourself: Each time you go to the mall or have thirty minutes to kill while you're waiting for that hairstylist who's running behind schedule, try to find one gift for someone on your list.

Besides the specific names on your list, you'll also want to have some "backup gifts" wrapped under the tree for unexpected guests who stop by with a present for you, and for any oversights (which inevitably happen). These gifts should be as universally applicable as possible, such as the *mature traditional* "standards" we discussed in Chapters Seven and Eight.

If you have children, establish a holiday ritual with them that also provides you with free labor! When I was a child, one of the most anticipated days of the year was the Friday after Thanksgiving. This was the day when all the trunks and boxes of Christmas decorations were brought down from the attic! Mom and I would decorate the entire house and then sit in front of the lit tree listening to Christmas music. Mom, my sister Paula and I would make regular treks to the mall and excitedly come home to wrap our treasures. Mom and Paula were always better "wrappers" than I, but together we got the job done. I now bring that same exuberance to my own home at Christmastime.

So find ways to make the holidays fun, special and festive. Deploy systems to stay organized. Delegate responsibility and distribute the workload. Be prepared by stocking up on necessary supplies. And start early!

chapter sixteen

thank-you
notes

Whenever you receive a gift it is non-negotiable to send a thank-you note, ideally handwritten. Graciousness never goes out of style. It may seem old-fashioned in this day and age of e-mail and text messaging, but it's just the right thing to do. So invest in some nice stationery (which is why I recommend it as a great gift idea in Chapter Seven), and don't procrastinate when it comes to this all-important task. After all, even celebs such as Bette Midler, Heather Locklear, Sharon Stone, Allison Janney, Jill Scott, Jenna Elfman, Erika Christensen, Lauren Holly, Debra Messing, Megan Mullally, Deidre Hall and Lee Ann

Womack are very good about sending their thank-you notes!

Here are the basic ingredients to keep in mind when writing a thank-you note. Let's face it, if you're going to give fabulous gifts, shouldn't you also write fabulous thank-you notes? I'll answer for you . . . Yes!

- Specifically reference the gift you received.
- State why it was special and appreciated.
- Mention when or how you plan to use the gift.
- Describe the emotion you felt when you received the present.
- Keep your note casual and avoid overly formal or archaic language. You want your note to sound like you, not Charlotte Bronte.
- Compliment the person on their generosity, kindness, thoughtfulness or whatever descriptive word comes to mind.
- Don't go overboard in terms of gushiness (unless it's consistent with your personality/behavior). You want to seem sincere.
- Mail your note in a timely fashion. It's not only good etiquette, it also lets the person know that their gift arrived. Although you may have a year after a wedding to pony up a gift, you

should send out a thank-you note within one month of receiving the present. Don't procrastinate . . . the sooner the better. The longer you wait, the more likely you'll forget to send the note.

At the end of the day, anything is better than no note at all. So whether it's a one-line postcard that says "Thanks for the great gift," an e-mail or a phone message, keep a list of each present you receive (especially at high-volume gift times like birthdays, weddings and Christmas) and systematically send some sort of acknowledgment.

Here's a sample you can use as a template:

Dear Aunt Helen,

The gourmet cooking spices you gave me for my birthday will be put to great use at one of my upcoming dinner parties. As you know, I love to cook . . . so your gift was perfect! It was so nice of you to remember me in such a thoughtful way.

Much love,
Lash

Most of the celebrity thank-you notes I receive are short and to the point. They often reflect the personality of the star sending the correspondence. Without violating their privacy, here is the actual text from three of my most treasured thank-you notes from three of my favorite celebrity "friends":

Dear Lash,
Ooh—the boots rock! Thank you for the goodies. Actually better than goodies! Thank you for thinking of me on my birthday!

Dear Lash,
Thank you so very much for my gift basket. It is so beyond great! I have never been so excited to go through each and every nook and cranny! Thanks again.

Dear Lash,
I'm still looking thru your wonderful gift. Thank you for your kindness and all the fab swag. Best wishes on your newest endeavor!!

And then there's the thank-you gift. If someone makes an extraordinary gesture or goes well out of their way to do you a favor, a thank-you note may not be a strong enough gesture. Even if it's a small gift or simply a beautiful floral delivery, the classy thing to do is reward acts of kindness with acts of appreciation. Positive reinforcement is the best way I've found to keep the favors coming!

chapter seventeen

giving
for the
soul

The "joy of giving" may sound quite cliché. However, like most clichés, the actual experience is much more profound than mere words could ever convey. Learning to give as a way of life helps you become a better partner, spouse, friend, employer and human being. It exemplifies a certain generosity that transcends the price tag of the item. It's a giving of time, of energy, of thought, of love.

One of the reasons I love gifts so much is that they have the ability to imbue both the giver and the receiver with a sense of fulfillment. Is it, in fact, better to give than to receive? It's somewhat of a trick question, as the real query is "Better for whom?"

I was recently asked to donate some items to a teenage girl (we'll call her Pam) who was suffering from a fatal disease. The doctors had given Pam a matter of weeks to live. A work associate of mine called to say that Pam's parents were very poor, and she wondered if I might be willing to assemble and donate a few items to make Pam's last days as enjoyable as possible. I put together a basket of goodies that any young girl would love, including beauty products, clothing, purses, games and jewelry. My colleague picked up the gift basket and extended her heartfelt thanks. A little over a week later I learned that Pam had passed away but that she hadn't stopped smiling that entire final week as she went through her gifts over and over again . . . applying the makeup, playing dress-up, swapping out accessories. To know that I touched someone's life in such a profound way was the real gift. I actually thanked my colleague for providing *me* that opportunity.

Gifts transcend need, fame and age. One of the greatest surprises in my professional life has been witnessing how celebrities light up when you give them a gift. Yes, many are actors who might "act" gracious and polite under most circumstances, but the childlike energy that is released when they receive a gift is not feigned. They demonstrate that sentiment sung so beautifully by the incomparable Barbra Streisand:

"We're all just people." People who at our core need to be loved, acknowledged, appreciated and remembered. *That* is the true power of a gift. If you give from love and not from obligation, both you and the recipient will experience the mutual reward.

A question I'm often asked during interviews related to our award show gift baskets is why we would give gifts to people who are already so wealthy. I always say that the basis of this question is a confusion of "need" with "gratitude." We are simply saying thank you to people who are donating their time free of charge to these events. You don't cease to be eligible for gratitude simply because you're rich and famous.

More important, so many of these celebrities give more to various charities than most people realize. Likewise, my company supports dozens of philanthropies by auctioning off items from our celebrity gift baskets, by having charity donors bid on the right to be pampered like an award show presenter and by volunteering our production services at various events. I'm proud to say that Distinctive Assets has helped raise tens of thousands of dollars for various charities over the years. We do so because we can, because it's the right thing to do and because it feels good to do it. It brings the cycle of giving and receiving full circle.

It's often a privilege to be able to utilize the generosity of the celebrities with whom I cross paths to raise funds for worthy causes. For example, I've assisted the Avon Breast Cancer Crusade launch three highly successful charity auctions over the years. I secured items ranging from "little black dresses" from stars' closets to celebrity lip imprints to help "Kiss Goodbye to Breast Cancer." Over twenty actresses have participated over the years, including Jenna Elfman, Debra Messing, Christina Aguilera, Jennifer Love Hewitt, Brooke Shields, Cybill Shepherd, Leah Remini, Kathy Najimy, Whoopi Goldberg, Patti LaBelle and Sharon Stone.

A tradition I started a few Christmases ago (thanks to my friend Anthony) is answering "Dear Santa" letters from underprivileged children. The first year, we went to the local post office and picked up unclaimed letters written to Santa Claus and addressed to the North Pole. We read through them and put the most deserving ones in a large fishbowl. At my annual holiday party, everyone who wanted to participate pulled out a letter and bought whatever was on the child's wish list (and if they had requested something unreasonable like a spaceship, they would get a toy rocket set or something that represented the desired item). We then delivered the presents on Christmas morning. Because I always stay in town for Christmas, I offered to deliver any of the gifts from people who wanted to participate but would be out of town on Christmas Day. Over the years, we've repeated this process many times and even "adopted" an entire classroom of deserving students at a local elementary school who would not have had many Christmas presents to open otherwise.

If you don't have the time or resources for an activity of that magnitude, find something you can do. Oscar-winner Angelina Jolie once said in an interview, "If you make twenty million dollars, you'll never miss it if you give ten million dollars away." Although most of us don't make twenty million dollars or even one million dollars, we can all do something *we'll never miss*: donate those clothes we've outgrown to a women's shelter, skip our latte and give $5 to a local AIDS charity, throw our loose change into the Salvation Army bucket or simply say hello to a homeless person on the street and give them our leftovers as we're leaving a restaurant.

If you doubt the power of giving, try a little test. When you are feeling down or low, pick up a small token gift for someone you love. Give them the present "just because" and see what happens. I've found gift giving to be a highly effective antidepressant!

Sometimes the best presents are given for no reason at all. Surprise your best friend or spouse with an arrangement of flowers on a rainy Monday. Send your mother a note in the mail on a beautiful piece of stationery that says "Just wanted you to know that I was thinking about you." Having "occasions" makes us forget that *every* day we're alive and loved is reason enough to celebrate with a fabulous gift.

about the author

Lash Fary is founder & president of Distinctive Assets, a Los Angeles–based entertainment marketing company that has set new standards for "giving and receiving" through their coveted Gift Baskets and Gift Lounges for events such as the GRAMMY Awards, the Tony Awards, the People's Choice Awards, the Academy of Country Music Awards, the NAACP Image Awards, the MTV Movie Awards and the Kids' Choice Awards.

Lash is a frequent "expert guest" on fashion and gifting on a wide range of television shows. He is also quoted regularly in publications such as *USA Today, Variety, Los Angeles Times* and *Entertainment Weekly*. Lash provides his gift expertise to corporations, studios, celebrities and private clients nationwide. His gifting prowess has earned him the apt moniker: "The Gift Fary."

More information on Lash, Distinctive Assets and *Fabulous Gifts* is available at www.distinctive-assets.com.